JUDAISM, THE MESSIAH, AND JEWISH IDENTITY

Aaron Dranoff

© Copyright 2022 by Aaron Dranoff. All rights reserved.
Published by The Torah Guide LLC
Revised in 2023

The Torah Guide LLC.
TheTorahGuide.com

No part of this book may be reproduced in any form without written permission from The Torah Guide LLC.

In no way is it legal to reproduce, duplicate, or transmit any part of this document in either electronic means or in printed format. Recording of this publication is strictly prohibited and any storage of this document is not allowed unless with written permission from the publisher. All rights reserved.

The information provided herein is stated to be truthful and consistent, in that any liability, in terms of inattention or otherwise, by any usage or abuse of any policies, processes, or directions contained within is the solitary and utter responsibility of the recipient reader. Under no circumstances will any legal responsibility or blame be held against the publisher for any reparation, damages, or monetary loss due to the information herein, either directly or indirectly.

Scripture quotations taken from the (NASB®) New American Standard Bible®, Copyright © 1960, 1971, 1977, 1995, 2020 by The Lockman Foundation. Used by permission. All rights reserved. www.lockman.org

Where the NASB uses LORD or Lord GOD in small caps to translate the Hebrew tetragrammaton (YHWH), the author has substituted the actual tetragrammaton instead. This notice replaces the use of square brackets to indicate all such substitutions.

Contents

Introduction 1
1. The Function of the Written Torah in Jewish Identity 3
2. Origins of Rabbinic Judaism 25
3. The Oral Torah Examined 49
4. Judaism According to the Tanakh 69
5. The Tanakh and the New Testament 101
6. Common Concerns 145
Conclusion.. 169
How to Find References.. 171
Bibliography.. 173
Endotes.. 177

Introduction

Growing up, I always struggled with my Jewish identity. The fact that I was Jewish was clearly very important to my parents, but it was frustrating for me. My parents used to be agnostic Jews. This made for an interesting family dynamic, which becomes even stranger once I tell you that my agnostic Jewish parents took me to church growing up.

The story I was told is that when my older brother was about six years old (which made me one), he told my parents he believed in Jesus. My agnostic Jewish parents told him, "Oh no, honey, we don't believe in Jesus. We're Jewish." To which my brother replied, "That's okay because he lives in my heart." After that, my parents became curious about Jesus and started going to church with our neighbors. They went in part because they had some questions and in part for the community.

My parents always insisted I was Jewish, but since they were taking me to church regularly I didn't fully know what that meant. I knew that to be a Christian you needed to believe in Jesus. At the time I thought that believing in Jesus meant being convinced he was a real historical figure, and I did think he was a real person. So, even though I didn't truly believe in Jesus or follow him I thought that made me a Christian.

At the same time when I explained this to my Jewish friends, they would tell me I wasn't Jewish. Then when I was in high school my family stopped going to church and other than Pesach religion was not on my radar anymore. While I was in college I became more and more involved in the Jewish community, and I started having spiritual questions. These questions turned into a rigorous search for truth.

I originally just wanted to be certain that there was no God because I wanted to live my life my own way and not have to worry about it. I expected that hardly any evidence would point to a God. What I found shocked me. Not only is there reliable early evidence in various forms, but when you weigh all the evidence, it overwhelmingly shows that Jesus is the Jewish Messiah.

Growing up, one of the main reasons I was confused about my Jewish identity was because I didn't understand the Jewishness of Jesus's mission. What I began to understand is that Jesus—or Yeshua, as he would have been called in Hebrew—was as Jewish as it gets."

Not only that, but all his disciples were Jewish, and almost all the New Testament authors were as well. And none of them ever forfeited their Jewish identity or converted to another religion. Rather, they saw Yeshua as the fulfillment of Judaism, and they believed that the rescue he offers extends not only to the Jewish people but to everyone.

The question is, Who is right: the majority of Jewish people today who don't think Yeshua is the Messiah or those who believe he is?

This book is an analysis of the history and validity of both schools of thought. It should be taken as part of the discussion between two different schools of thought within Judaism. The goal is to uncover the correct understanding of the Hebrew Bible, and is therefore done with a deep respect for Judaism and Jewish people. Understanding the relationship between Judaism and the Messiah is key to understanding what it means to be Jewish. Once we understand what the God of Israel intended Judaism to be, the Jewish way of life starts to become compelling, even irresistible.

1

The Function of the Written Torah in Jewish Identity

In this chapter we will explore the origins of the Jewish people. We'll focus on the connection and importance of the written Torah to their identity. We're investigating the function and significance of the written Torah according to the written Torah.

This book will make three claims about what the Torah is intended to be to the Jewish people:
1. The Torah is meant to be a written record of what God has done for the Jewish people.
2. The Torah is a written document that serves as the *sole contract* between the nation of Israel and their God.
3. According to the biblical authors, God expects Jewish people to shape their whole life around the Torah.

The Torah's Function as Historical Record

The Jewish people are one of the oldest cohesive people groups around today. Not only have they lasted as a distinct people, but they have accomplished this in spite of multiple exiles and spending thousands of years dispersed all over the earth with no land, military, or even an official governing body of their own.[1] More than just lacking a home country for the majority of their existence, the Jewish people have been targeted and attacked almost everywhere they've tried set up camp.[2] There's no other nation still around with a similar story.

It's commonly thought that the Jewish people have been able to maintain their nationhood throughout this adversity by resisting assimilation and fighting to hold on to their Jewish identity. So, what is Jewish identity? We're going to explore what it is, where it comes from, and whether there is or isn't a "Jewish way of life."

Essentially, we'll ask, What does it mean to be Jewish, and should I let my Jewishness affect how I live my life?

The Jewish people have carefully preserved a collection of ancient scrolls that represents their self-understanding through the lens of their earliest history.[3] We call this collection the *Torah*: the five books of Moses that begin the Hebrew Bible. Jewish identity originated with the events and ideas taught in the Torah, so any supposed guide for the Jewish people would be lacking if it didn't begin with a look at the Torah and the God of Israel.[4] Although most Jewish people today wouldn't consider themselves Torah observant, most are no doubt aware of the ancient text that claims to contain the early history of their people.[5]

This guide explores whether there is a right way to be Jewish by studying the origins and development of the Jewish people. The Torah contains early narratives about the beginning of the Jewish people and their purpose. Its authors have included for us a claim about the Torah's place in a Jewish person's life.

It's outside the scope of this guide to prove the validity of the Torah or the Hebrew Bible. Instead, this book is going to accept the Torah as a set of ancient records. It will assume that the authors were truthful and also assume that the biblical God is real. If you don't agree with those assumptions, I think this book will still be a useful study into the development of Jewish heritage, especially what their sacred texts teach about our people. Believe in the God of ancient Israel or not, the Torah contains the self-understanding of the Jewish people since ancient times, and we can't make a genuine attempt at understanding Jewish identity without it.[6]

We don't have to guess what kind of literature the Torah was intended to be. In the narrative, the authors give us clear details about why it was written. The first place where the Torah mentions its own writing is in Exodus chapter 17. Starting in verse 8, you will see that Moses is commanded to record how YHWH has just delivered them from the Amalekites, an enemy the Israelites couldn't defeat on their own. YHWH tells Moses, write this down, and he gives Moses the reason why: so Israel will have a record of what happened. God wanted Israel to always remember that he saved them, so that they would trust that he will continue to save them. "Then YHWH said to Moses, 'Write this in a book as a memorial and recite it to Joshua, that I will utterly wipe out the memory of Amalek from under heaven'" (Exodus 17:14–15).[1]

One of the ways the Torah is intended to be understood then, is as a written record of what God did for the Jewish people. Let's dive into the Torah and see what it has to say about what God did for his people and what it means to be Jewish.

Setting the Stage: Creation through Abraham (Genesis 1–11)

This chapter is about the function and importance of the written Torah to the Jewish people. To understand the Torah's role in Jewish life, we need to have a basic grasp of the plot by the time we meet the first Jew in chapters 11 and 12. So let's take a look at the basic storyline.

---
[1] Throughout this book, where the NASB uses LORD or Lord GOD in small caps to translate the Hebrew tetragrammaton (YHWH), I have substituted YHWH. This notice avoids the repeated and distracting use of brackets to indicate the substitution.

Genesis 1 opens with a time before Jews, a time before Abraham, all the way back in the very beginning with the creation of the universe. Over the course of six days, God takes a wild, chaotic universe and puts it in order so that it is a place hospitable for human life.[7] This creation story culminates on the seventh day, when God stops creating and, together, God and humans rest and reign over the earth (Gen. 1:26).

If we track the use of the word "good" (*tov* in Hebrew) through Genesis 1, we'll notice something important. On almost every day that God created, he saw that what he created was good.

> Then God said, "Let there be light"; and there was light. God saw that the light was good; and God separated the light from the darkness. (Gen. 1:3–4)

What becomes apparent is that every time God created something beneficial for human life, he saw that it was good (vv. 4, 10, 12, 18, 21, 25). Then when God created humans on the sixth day, God saw that what he had created was "very good" (v. 31). Up until this point, God is not only the provider of everything good, but he is also the one who decides what is good and what is not good: "Then YHWH God said, "It is not good for the man to be alone." (Gen. 2:18).

In Genesis 2, you'll see that Adam and Eve are in the beautiful garden God created. There he gave them many good things and many trees to eat from. (vv. 9, 16). God also gave the humans a choice. To represent this choice, he put two trees in the garden. One is called the tree of life; the other, the tree of the knowledge of good and evil (v. 9). We've seen that God is the one who decides what is good and what is bad, so of these two main trees, the tree of life seems like the better option. But if the choice wasn't clear enough, God explicitly told the humans, "From any tree of the garden you may freely eat; but from the tree of the knowledge of good and evil you shall not eat, for on the day that you eat from it you will certainly die" (v. 16).

At this point in the record, we see that God is the one who has been providing everything that's good, and he decides what is good and what is not good. The things that he deems good have always been beneficial to human life, and things that are detrimental to humans he deems not good. But for some reason, God wants to give humans the freedom to choose to trust him or to trust themselves. So, he created two trees to represent that choice and tells them not to choose the tree of knowledge of good and evil, the tree that represents knowing good and evil for oneself instead of trusting what God says is good and evil.

In Genesis 3, after being convinced by a new and deceptive figure, the woman eats from the tree. Adam condones her action and eats as well. And for the first time, the phrase that has previously only been used to describe God's perspective we now see used to show the woman's:

> When the woman saw that the tree was good for food, and that it was a delight to the eyes, and that the tree was desirable to make one wise, she took some of its fruit and ate. (Gen. 3:6)

The woman saw that the tree was "good for food"—but was it really? God said Adam and Eve shouldn't eat from it, and we will see, from the consequences of their doing so, that the tree was in fact *not* good. The point is that the woman did not trust God to decide what was good and to provide it; instead, *she* decided what was good and what was not good, and she took the fruit. In chapter 3, for the first time, we see a human choose to define good for themselves and take that "good" thing instead of receiving God's abundant and truly good provision.

After Adam and Eve took the fruit, God confronted them and told them more details about the consequence of their sin. There are two key points to focus on in the sentence he imposed on them. The first is this: "You are dust, and to dust you shall return" (Gen. 3:19). This is the climax of the curse, or consequence, it's a poetic way of repeating to them that humans will now die because, in providing for themselves and deciding what was good and what was not, they tried to take God's place.

Not only will humans die, but God also sends them away from his presence, the garden of Eden (v. 23). We begin to see that once humans sin, they are no longer able to be in the presence of God.

The second point is this: Within the bad news, God also gives Adam and Eve some good news. It comes in two parts. First, the humans aren't going to die immediately. "In pain shall you bear children," God tells Eve (v. 16). So they will have offspring. Second, there will be some sort of conflict between the seed of the woman and the seed of the deceptive figure. And somehow, though he'll be struck back in the process, one of the woman's offspring is going to strike a blow to the deceptive figure's head:

> "I will make enemies
> Of you and the woman,
> And of your offspring and her Descendant;
> He shall bruise you on the head,
> And you shall bruise Him on the heel."
>
> (Gen. 3:15)

Even though God sent the humans away from his presence because of sin, he told them he would take care of the sin problem by using the offspring of the woman to defeat the deceiver.

Remember that literature is just communication in written form. The Torah is communicating something to us. If we want to correctly understand what it is telling us through its narrative, we need to follow the story arc. The Torah begins with God creating the world, creating humans, and ruling his creation together with them. Conflict arose when humans rebelled against God. But even as God was telling them their punishment and banishing them from his presence because of the evil they did, he already had a plan to restore them and all creation to the way he intended it.

After the human failure in chapter 3, and God's hint of a future deliverance, the sin problem got worse and worse as more humans inhabited the earth. "Now it came about, when man began to multiply on the face of the land ... YHWH saw that the wickedness of mankind was great on the earth" (Gen. 6:1, 5).

God saw the evil on the earth, and because he loved his creation, he took it seriously and removed it by wiping humans off the earth—humans are the vehicle for spreading evil. But since God also loves humans, he didn't destroy evil without a rescue plan for them. This time he used Noah and an ark (Gen. 6–8).

Even though God had wiped evil off the earth, he preserved a remnant of humanity. So very quickly humanity repeats the failure of the garden and continues their evil (Gen. 9:21–28). Remember, God had instructed humans to fill the earth. But, in chapter 11 we read about a nation that deliberately rebelled against that command and hatched a plan to try and make sure God didn't scatter them (Gen. 11:4). God thwarted their plan and forced them to spread around the earth.

In a nutshell, then: Chapters 1–11 of Genesis describe God's plan for humans and how the first couple subsequently turned against him, bringing evil into the world. The narrative then shows people repeating this evil in each generation, demonstrating that all humanity keeps bringing evil into creation. It is at this point in the story that the origins of the Jewish people begin, with the appearance of Abraham the patriarch.

Abraham, the Patriarch of the Jewish People

Abram (later called Abraham) is introduced in chapter 11 in a genealogy tracking the woman's descendents, and he takes center stage abruptly in chapter 12 as the story changes gears. From that point, it is evident that Abram is part of God's plan to defeat the deceiver's influence over creation and undo the curses humans brought on creation and themselves. Here is what YHWH said to Abram:

> "Go from your country,
> And from your relatives
> And from your father's house,
> To the land which I will show you;
> And I will make you into a great nation,
> And I will bless you,
> And make your name great;

And you shall be a blessing;
And I will bless those who bless you,
And the one who curses you I will curse.
And in you all the families of the earth will be blessed."

(Gen. 12:1–3)

Right away YHWH promised Abram great things and many blessings, but he went even further. His promise "In you all the families of the earth will be blessed" shows that God wants to bless the world as a whole by using this one man and his descendants, who would eventually become a nation, the Nation of Israel. Biblical scholars Moshe Weinfeld and Robert Alter note that after the curses given in chapter 3:14-19, history reached a turning point with Abraham as God promised to undo the curses and replace them with the blessings promised in chapter 12:1–3. A string of curses came to all of creation because of sin, but a string of blessings came through the family God would use to bless all creation.[8]

Let's retrace the plot. God created a good world in which he provided good things for humans in abundance, God being the one who decides what is good and evil. God and humans ruled the world together for a time until humans became convinced they should take the position of God and decide for themselves what is good and evil. Their choice resulted in a string of curses on them and the land (creation), and God sent them away from his presence. But he hinted at taking care of the problem of evil that humans brought to his creation. The evil worsened as more humans were born. Then a man named Abram, the father of the Jewish people, was introduced to the story. Abram appeared to be the man through whom God planned to undo the curses Adam and Eve brought to creation.

—

This book is an exploration of what it means to be Jewish. We are starting with a basic overview of the major story arc of the Bible for one reason. As we just saw, the Bible doesn't begin with Abraham, let alone any Jewish people at all. Abraham, the father of the Jewish people, is introduced after a lot has already happened.

Like most stories, this narrative begins with everything at peace. Then there is a conflict with a promised resolution. Abram is then introduced as the first step toward that resolution. As we might have already noticed, the primary language of this conflict and resolution in the Torah is "curses" and "blessing." Humans introduced curses or conflict into the world; God will use humans, specifically Abram and his descendants, to remove the curse and restore blessing—bring resolution—to all the nations of the earth. When you see "blessing" in the Torah, the authors were probably invoking the language about undoing the curses brought to creation.

According to the record written down in the Torah, we can see that the Jewish people, beginning with Abraham, have a function. That function is to bring blessing to the world. Blessing for the nations is the reason that the Torah focuses on Abraham. It's also the reason that the story then zooms in on his son Isaac and then Jacob. The promise to bless the nations through these individuals and their offspring is repeated time and time again so we can make no mistake about what God is using them for (Gen. 12:3; 18:18; 22:18; 26:4-5; 28:14). The Jewish people are the first step in God's plan to get the evil out of his world and restore humans to their proper place as corulers under his authority.

According to its authors, the first purpose of the Torah is to provide recorded history. As you continue to follow the narrative within of Abraham and his descendants, you'll see subconflict arise. In the subconflict, this nation to whom God promised blessing found themselves in a foreign land, enslaved (Ex. 2:23). The story continues in the book of Exodus with God freeing the Israelites—Abraham's descendants—from slavery and making a formal contract with them.

The Torah's Function as the Only Contract between the Nation of Israel and Their God

Israel's Unique Relationship with God

In the second book of the Torah, we get a fuller picture of who the Jewish people are. We see God inviting the people of Israel into a unique relationship with himself through a covenant agreement.

> "'Now then, if you will indeed obey My voice and keep My covenant, then you shall be My own possession among all the peoples, for all the earth is Mine; and you shall be to Me a kingdom of priests and a holy nation.' These are the words that you shall speak to the sons of Israel." (Ex. 19:5–6)

God tells them, If you keep my covenant, then you will get these blessings and be "a kingdom of priests." All the people accept the proposal: "Then all the people answered together and said, 'All that YHWH has spoken we shall do'" (Ex. 19:8). In the following chapters 21–23, YHWH tells Moses all the covenant terms He expects them to follow if they accept. Then they reaffirm their acceptance (Exodus 24:4–7).

The second time the writing of the Torah is mentioned is in Exodus 24, which gives a fuller picture of what the Torah is supposed to be to the Jewish people. In addition to being a historical record of the Jewish people and what God has done for them, it is now also a contract.

> Moses wrote down all the words of YHWH. . . .Then he took the Book of the Covenant and read it as the people listened; and they said, "All that YHWH has spoken we will do, and we will be obedient!" (Ex. 24:4, 7)

What words from YHWH did Moses write down? He wrote everything included in the conditional contract, every law.

Every Agreement Was Written Down

Now the Torah is functioning as more than just a historical record of the Jewish people and what God has done for them. It is also a written contract between God and his people: "Moses wrote down all the words of YHWH." According to the Torah and the whole Hebrew Bible, the entirety of the covenant was written down. (The Torah is even called the Book of the Covenant in Exodus 24:7.)

> So Moses wrote this Law [Torah] and gave it to the priests, the sons of Levi who carried the ark of the covenant of YHWH, and to all the elders of Israel. Then Moses commanded them, saying, "At the end of every seven years, at the time of the year of the release of debts, at the Feast of Booths, when all Israel comes to appear before YHWH your God at the place which He will choose, you shall read this Law before all Israel so that they hear it. Assemble the people, the men, the women, the children, and the stranger who is in your town, so that they may hear and learn and fear YHWH your God, and be careful to follow all the words of this Law." (Deuteronomy 31:9–12)

This is strong evidence that, according to the Torah, the entirety of the Torah was written down. In other words, the Torah is claiming that it is the whole contract God gave to Moses, written down. According to this passage, there was not any part of the law that was not written down. How do we know that? It says that Moses wrote down the Torah and that every seven years the priests were charged with reading the Torah to all Israel. Why would the priests read it to Israel? Well, it tells us why: "So that they may hear and learn and fear YHWH your God, and be careful to do all the words of this Law [Torah]." In other words, if the people heard the Torah *read to them*, they would be able to keep all the words of the Torah. That means there were no rules the people needed to keep that were not written down. How else could all the laws be read?

In Deuteronomy 12:32, God warns Israel not to add or remove any laws from the Torah: "Whatever I command you, you shall be careful to do; you shall not add to nor take anything away from it." So the Torah serves as a written covenant, or contract, that tells us that everything God commanded the people of Israel to do was written down in the book of the Torah. Not only did the authors of the Torah record that the entirety of the Law was written down in the Torah, but the contract or covenant itself leaves no room for any new laws: "You shall not add to the word which I am commanding you, nor take away from it, so that you may keep the commandments of YHWH your God which I am commanding you" (Deut. 4:2). The Torah teaches that everything God and Israel agreed on was written down and that no new laws would be valid under the covenant within.

Now let's take a look at two passages in the Hebrew Bible that occur after the Torah. This will clue us in to what very early Israel thought about what the Torah was.

> Then afterward he read all the words of the Law, the blessing and the curse, according to everything that is written in the Book of the Law. There was not a word of all that Moses had commanded which Joshua did not read before all the assembly of Israel with the women, the little ones, and the strangers who were living among them. (Joshua 8:34–35)

Joshua was the first leader after Moses passed away, and very early on in his leadership career, he read all the words of the Torah. Furthermore, the author makes it abundantly clear that everything God commanded Moses was written down. We know all of it was written down because he says, "There was not a word of all that Moses had commanded which Joshua did not read before all the assembly of Israel." What exactly was Joshua reading? Could it have been notes that he prepared before his speech? No, the author is overly explicit that Joshua was reading the book of the Torah. And he is equally as clear that the book of the Torah contains absolutely every word that Moses instructed the people of Israel to follow. So, we already know that the Torah considered itself the only contract between God and the people of Israel. Now we see that this is a consistent position in the Hebrew Bible, even as it continues past the Torah.

If we move forward in the Hebrew Bible to a later time in Israel's history, to the death bed of the famous King David, we'll see what he thinks about the Torah.

> "I am going the way of all the earth. So be strong, and prove yourself a man. Do your duty to YHWH your God, to walk in His ways, to keep His statutes, His commandments, His ordinances, and His testimonies, according to what is written in the Law [Torah] of Moses, so that you may succeed in all that you do and wherever you turn." (1 Kings 2:2–3)

If David's statement on his deathbed were the only place that the Hebrew Bible mentioned the covenant as a fully written-down text, it wouldn't be an airtight case. David only implies here that everything God commanded Moses was written down. He doesn't explicitly say it. But let's keep in mind that Exodus 24:7, Deuteronomy 31:9–13, and Joshua 8:34–35 all do explicitly state that everything God commanded Moses, Moses wrote down. So, when David heavily implies that the whole Torah was written down, it should be sufficient.

Furthermore, remember that these are David's last words to his son. He is telling Solomon what he thinks are the most important things for Solomon to know once David isn't around anymore. The thing that King David, the man God said is after his own heart (1 Sam.13:14), considers most important in life is to follow God's commands. And he tells Solomon where to find those commands; he tells him to look at the commands written down in the Torah.

So, if the Torah contains all the words God commanded Moses, and nobody is ever supposed to add new laws, then the question becomes, How can anything after the Torah be Scripture? This matters because we know that Scripture continues past the Torah section.

There is another name for the Hebrew Bible that will be helpful for us: the Tanakh.

TaNaK is a Hebrew acronym for the three collections that make up the Hebrew Bible: the Torah, the Prophets, and the Writings (Torah, Nevi'im, and Ketuvim in Hebrew). What do we do with the rest of these Scriptures if only the Torah commands are allowed?

According to the terms of the Torah, during the life of the covenant, any new candidate for Scripture must not add any new laws to the contract. If there are any new laws, it cannot not be a scriptural text (Deut.12:32; 4:2).

God used prophets to speak to his covenant people many times, and many of the messages God sent through his prophets were recorded in the Prophets and the Writings sections of the Tanakh. But when God spoke to his people through the prophets, he did not add any new laws. Rather, he was pleading with his disobedient people to turn back to the Law (Josh. 1:7; 1 Kings 2:3).

According to the Tanakh, from the time of Moses, the time of Joshua, and every subsequent generation recorded, Israel never kept all the laws of the covenant (see Num. 21:5; Josh. 7:11; Jer. 11:10, Neh. 1:6-7). The covenant between God and the people of Israel was conditional. If they kept all the laws, then they would get all the blessings promised; if they did not keep all the laws, then they would receive all the curses (Deut.28:1–2, 13–14, 15, 58). The Torah is very clear that there would be a very serious penalty if the Israelites did not keep all of the laws.

But we see in the Prophets that God is very patient (2 Chron. 36:15–16), even though every generation is recorded as not only breaking some of the laws but actually breaking most of them. God sent messages through Prophets to give them many chances. The Prophets and the Writings do not add any new laws to the Torah; they instead contain God's warnings to the people to stop breaking the laws given in the Torah. This is why they can be regarded as Scripture. God commanded the people to not add any new laws to his laws, but none of the Prophets or the Writings added new laws. Even God himself doesn't add laws in the Prophets or the Writings; he just sends messages telling the people to start following all the laws he gave in the Torah.

Upon reading the Tanakh, it eventually becomes clear that the people of Israel usually didn't listen to the prophets and kept breaking the laws. As a result, God sent them away from his land, and they received the promised curses.

> Yet YHWH, the God of their fathers, sent word to them again and again by His messengers, because He had compassion on His people and on His dwelling place; but they continually mocked the messengers of God, despised His words, and scoffed at His prophets, until the wrath of YHWH rose against His people, until there was no remedy. (2 Chron. 36:15–16; cf. Jer. 8:5–6; 19:3–6; Ezek. 2:3)

This cause and effect is a pattern identical to that of Adam and Eve. They didn't trust God to decide what was right and wrong, so they made the decision to disobey God. And because they chose to disobey God, he sent them away from his presence—Adam and Eve from Eden; the Israelites from Israel.

Just as God had a plan to restore his creation when Adam and Eve sinned, and just as God dealt with the sin problem in Noah's time, with a plan to rescue humans through Noah, so also God told the sinning people of Israel that he would save them from their sin problem as well. The Prophets gave more details about the snake-bruising descendant of Eve (Gen.3:15), proclaiming the hopeful future of a reigning king who would usher in a new kingdom where there will be no evil or sadness.

> The people who walk in darkness
> Will see a great light;
> Those who live in a dark land,
> The light will shine on them. . . .
> For a Child will be born to us, a Son will be given to us;
> And the government will rest on His shoulders;
> And His name will be called Wonderful Counselor, Mighty God,

> Eternal Father, Prince of Peace.
> There will be no end to the increase of His government or of peace
> On the throne of David and over his kingdom,
> To establish it and to uphold it with justice and righteousness
> From then on and forevermore.
> The zeal of YHWH of armies will accomplish this.
>
> (Isa. 9:2, 6–7)[2]

And moreover, we get a glimpse that suffering will be gone in this new kingdom

> "For behold, I create new heavens and a new earth;
> And the former things will not be remembered or come to mind.
> But be glad and rejoice forever in what I create;
> For behold, I create Jerusalem for rejoicing
> And her people for gladness.
> I will also rejoice in Jerusalem and be glad in My people;
> And there will no longer be heard in her
> The voice of weeping and the sound of crying."
>
> (Isa. 65:17–19)

The Prophets and the Writings contain warnings from God to Israel to stop breaking the law, and they continue to record the history of the Jewish people. The record included in the Tanakh specifically tracks God's plan to use the people of Israel as an instrument for undoing the curses that Adam and Eve brought to creation. And the Prophets proclaim the hopeful future of a reigning king who will restore Israel to a new world with no sin and suffering.

So, we can see how the Prophets and the Writings are not in

---

[2] From the Prophets section of the TaNaK, 740–700 BCE. See Skolnik, *Encyclopaedia Judaica*, vol. 10, 58.

conflict with the Torah but are built on the foundation of the Torah. This shows why the Hebrew Bible is referred to by the acronym TaNaK. The Torah remained the only contract between the people of Israel and the God of Israel given to Moses. The Prophets and the Writings do not claim to be a new contract or contain anything that would suggest any new laws or detractions. After the Israelites broke the Mt. Sinai covenant, God promised through the Prophets to fix it by making a new covenant that is unbreakable. We'll explore this idea later, but to introduce the thought:

> "Behold, days are coming," declares YHWH, "when I will sow the house of Israel and the house of Judah with the seed of mankind and the seed of animals. . . .
>
> "Behold, days are coming," declares YHWH, "when I will make a new covenant with the house of Israel and the house of Judah, not like the covenant which I made with their fathers on the day I took them by the hand to bring them out of the land of Egypt, My covenant which they broke, although I was a husband to them," declares YHWH. "For this is the covenant which I will make with the house of Israel after those days," declares YHWH: "I will put My law within them and write it on their heart; and I will be their God, and they shall be My people. They will not teach again, each one his neighbor and each one his brother, saying, 'Know YHWH,' for they will all know Me, from the least of them to the greatest of them," declares YHWH, "for I will forgive their wrongdoing, and their sin I will no longer remember." (Jeremiah 31: 27, 31–34)

At this point, we know that during the Sinai[3] covenant everything commanded to Moses was written down. Jeremiah made these prophecies hundreds of years after Moses, during the Second Temple period, around 587 BCE.[9] According to Jeremiah's use of the future

---

[3] The covenant given to Moses via the Torah is sometimes referred to as the "Sinai Covenant."

tense, "Behold, days are coming," the Sinai covenant was still very much active during his time. But he talks about a future time when God will fix the problem that the Israelites created when they broke the Sinai covenant. Jeremiah ties it together with a time when Israel, the house of Judah, gentiles, and all creation will be united under a new covenant that is made possible through forgiveness.

The Torah Expects Your Life to Revolve Around it

According to the Tanakh, God instructs every Jewish person to shape their whole life around the written Torah. Once you understand that the Torah was written down to preserve the origins and history of the Jewish people and what God has done for them, as well as serving as a contract between God and Israel, it becomes clear why he expects that level of commitment. This idea is not totally absent from Judaism today. Rabbis teach that a Jewish person is supposed to recite the Shema every day, morning and night (Kitzur Shulchan Aruch 17). What is the Shema?

> "Hear, Israel, YHWH our God, YHWH is one. And you shall love YHWH your God with all your heart and with all your soul and with all your strength. These words, which I am commanding you today, shall be on your heart. And you shall repeat them diligently to your sons and speak of them when you sit in your house, when you walk on the road, when you lie down, and when you get up. You shall also tie them as a sign to your hand, and they shall be as frontlets on your forehead. You shall also write them on the doorposts of your house and on your gates." (Deut. 6:4–9)

The meaning of this passage is evident. Israelites, Jewish people, are expected to put their God first. How are they told to do that? By cherishing the words that God commanded them. They can find those words all written in the Torah (Ex. 24:7; Deut. 31:9–13; Josh. 8:34–35). So, the Shema teaches that they should cherish the words of the Torah, and teach them to their children, and talk about them no matter what they're doing. All day long a Jewish person is supposed to think about the Torah, according to the Shema, from when they wake up in the morning to before they sleep at night. The Shema teaches that the words of God are to guide a person at every moment. The imagery in the Shema is almost that the Torah should guide a person the way blinders guide a horse. The message is clear: The Torah sees itself as the most essential part of a Jewish person's life, so much so that it should dominate the life, and even the thoughts, of every Jewish person.

The very beginning of the first book of the Prophets, Joshua, hammers this point home as well.

> "Only be strong and very courageous; be careful to do according to all the Law [Torah] which Moses My servant commanded you; do not turn from it to the right or to the left, so that you may achieve success wherever you go. This Book of the Law shall not depart from your mouth, but you shall meditate on it day and night, so that you may be careful to do according to all that is written in it; for then you will make your way prosperous, and then you will achieve success." (Joshua 1:7–8)

This command is spoken by God directly to Joshua. The instruction here is that the way Joshua will be able to keep everything written in the Torah is to meditate on it day and night. When God told Joshua to meditate on it, as odd as it might sound, Joshua was promised success and prosperity if he became a Bible nerd and studied Torah every night and day.

In Psalm 1 we see that this idea is universalized. Psalm 1 intentionally uses the same language from Joshua 1. This time, however, the teaching is applied to any person.

> Blessed is the person who does not walk in the counsel of the wicked,
> Nor stand in the path of sinners,

Nor sit in the seat of scoffers!
But his delight is in the Law [Torah] of YHWH,
And on His Law he meditates day and night.
He will be like a tree planted by streams of water,
Which yields its fruit in its season,
And its leaf does not wither;
And in whatever he does, he prospers.

(Ps. 1:1–3)

The psalmist applies the blessing that God promised Joshua to anyone who studies the teaching of God, day and night. (*Torah* can also be translated as "teaching.")[10] It becomes clear that the authors of the Torah intended the five books of Moses to be the foundation and lifelong pursuit of every Jewish person's life.

Chapter 1: Summary

Part 1: The Torah is an ancient written document that serves as a record of what God has done for the Jewish people. It's their earliest history (Ex. 17:14-15).

1. What God has done for his people:
   a. God created a land for humans in which He provided good things in abundance, and He is the knower and decider of what is good and evil.
   b. Humans choose to decide what is good and evil for themselves, and instead of trusting God to provide, they take for themselves. This is an act of rebellion and introduces evil to creation.
   c. As humanity spreads, so does evil; the evil problem is coming from humans.
   d. Abraham is introduced as a fix for the evil problem that started in the garden. He and his descendants, Israel, are chosen to be a blessing to the world.

Part 2: The Torah is a written document that serves as the sole contract between the nation of Israel and their God (Ex. 24:7).

1. God invites these people into a unique relationship with himself (what it really means to be Jewish) (Ex. 19:4–6).

2. The Torah makes it evident that the entire agreement between God and Israel is recorded in the Torah. The Tanakh never mentions or condones any other laws or agreements while this one remains active.

3. God commanded that no one may add any commands to the written Torah.

4. It is the role of the priests to maintain that Torah (Jer. 2:8; 18:18; Mal. 2:7).

5. Neither the Prophets nor the Writings add laws, but they call

a disobedient people back to obedience.

Part 3: God expects every Jewish person to shape their whole life around the Torah (the Shema; Josh. 1:8; Psalm 1).

Conclusion: The Jewish people's identity is founded exclusively in the written Torah and its teachings. They are supposed to study the written Torah, without adding any additional commands, in order to know how to live as a Jew.

2

ORIGINS OF RABBINIC JUDAISM

Political Ascent

TIMELINE
This should help place the events we're going to discuss in Jewish History

~1750 BCE	~1200 BCE	515 BCE	167 BCE	~150 CE	70 CE
Abraham	Moses given the Torah	Second Temple Completed/ Hebrew Bible Finalized	Maccabean Revolt	Origins of the Pharisees	Second Temple Destroyed

Second Temple Period

We've firmly established that one function of the Torah is a contract that binds two parties, God and Israel, with all the laws that are exclusively recorded in the written Torah. The Torah makes that point clear over and over again. However, a small Jewish sect called the Pharisees appeared around 150 BCE that claimed there was more to the written law given to Moses at Sinai.[1] They claimed that God gave other parts of the Torah to Moses that Moses didn't write down but passed down orally[1]. The Pharisees later developed into a much bigger group known simply as rabbis.[2] The word *rabbi* just means "teacher," but it became the title of an official ordained position within later Pharisaic Judaism. To be a rabbi today is not just to be a Jewish teacher; it's to be ordained in accordance with the oral Law. We will track the origins of this group and their supposed oral law, some of what it teaches, and how other groups at the time viewed it. Then this chapter will show that the Judaism we are familiar with today does not come from the Sinai covenant between God and Israel, but that it actually comes from the man-made traditions of the Pharisees.

A vast library of Jewish literature was produced during the Second Temple period (516 BCE–70 CE). The Tanakh was finalized during this time and translated into Greek (called the Septuagint), the Maccabees were written, as were the Dead Sea Scrolls and much more.[3] Despite the vast body of Jewish religious literature that came out of this period, the Pharisees were never mentioned in any of it nor anywhere else until 150 BCE. There's no evidence of their group appearing any earlier.[4] The Pharisees' sect appeared in 150 BCE, and by 70 CE it had gained six thousand men, not a very impressive number.[5] Yet despite its small size, this group had strategically gained control of the Jewish people's political, legal, and religious lives by 70 CE.[6]

The Pharisees appeared around the same time as the Maccabean revolt. The Maccabean revolt was a heroic revolution led by the priestly family of the same name, Maccabees. The Greeks had taken over Israel during the previous century and then, under Antiochus III, began to desecrate Jewish temple worship beyond belief. The Greek's mockery of Jewish temple worship disgusted the Maccabees to the point that they revolted. They were inspired by a desire to honor God and keep his commandments (1 Macc. 1–2). Although their revolt was inspired out of selfless honor, the resulting dynasty, the Hasmonean Dynasty, quickly descended into a selfish power struggle. The Maccabees

---

[1] Chapters 2 and 3 analyze the relationship between the Hebrew Bible and oral Torah. So, in these chapters all Tanakh quotes will be written in bold to help avoid confusion.

installed members of their family as kings and even as high priest.

Given that the Pharisees appeared during this dynasty and were known for zealously keeping their religious traditions, the Pharisees likely developed in response to the quickly corrupted Hasmonean dynasty. And, similar to the Hasmonean dynasty, though their beginnings may have been honorable, the Pharisees quickly and successfully shifted their efforts toward gaining power for themselves.[7]

This guide attempts to show that Judaism as it is perceived today is not the same Judaism that was followed by our ancestors from the Sinai covenant through the Second Temple period. Since the fall of the Second Temple in 70 CE, people have associated Judaism with the man-made oral Torah. Not only does rabbinical Judaism today look different than Judaism did before the Pharisees, but the new "Judaism" is also in violation of the Sinai covenant. For clarity, in this guide I'll refer to Judaism as it is commonly understood today as "rabbinical Judaism" because Judaism today is led by rabbis through the oral law.

From 76–67 BCE, Queen Alexandra ruled over Israel as queen of the Hasmonean kingdom.[8] The Pharisees began to take control of Jewish life by aligning themselves with Queen Alexandra. Their control grew to such an extent that the first-century historian Josephus Flavius wrote:

> These Pharisees artfully insinuated themselves into her favor by little and little, and became themselves the real administrators of the public affairs: they banished and reduced whom they pleased; they bound and loosed [men] at their pleasure; and, to say all at once, they had the enjoyment of the royal authority.[9]

They infiltrated the government until they controlled it, to the extent of having all the royal authority, even over who is arrested or freed. Once they had control of the government ruling over Israel, they started to assert themselves and their theology over the religious lives of the Jewish people.

Religious Takeover

As you might have already picked up, the oral Torah was what distinguished the Pharisees from the rest of the Jewish people. During this time, the other Jewish sects, namely the Sadducees (priestly sect), the followers of Yeshua (Jesus), and the Essenes and Qumran society all rejected the oral Torah, arguing that the Pharisees had invented it themselves.[10]

Again, the Pharisees were a tiny group relative to the whole of the Jewish people. But by 70 BCE they had gained political power and many scholars think they had control of the Sanhedrin[11]. The Sanhedrin was a council of seventy-one men who had rule over religious decisions in Israel during this period. Both Sadducees and Pharisees sat on the Sanhedrin, and the two groups were constantly grappling for control[12].

Given the clarity in the Tanakh's teachings that adding to God's Law (Torah) was strictly forbidden, the Pharisees had a mountain to climb in proving the oral Torah's divine authority—especially because the oral Torah directly contradicts this written command by saying that "each generation must add new laws."[13]

According to the five books of Moses, the sole mediators between God and his people were the priests. Not even the king could take the duties of the priests (2 Chron. 26:19-21). The Pharisees saw the authority given to the priests in the written Torah, and they *took that power from the priests* by inserting their new oral Law. This power grab brings us right back to the first sin, in which Eve, instead of trusting that what God gave was good enough, took the power to decide good and evil for herself (Gen. 3:6). It's the same sin humanity has been replaying ever since the first two people. This time the consequence meant misleading the Jewish people for the past two millennia.

Justifying the Authority of the Oral Torah

How did the Pharisees try to validate their oral Torah if the Tanakh made it very clear that the entire Torah was written down and that there were no further laws? They had to find ways to prove an oral Torah by using the written Torah. Other Jewish groups during this time, namely the priests, Sadducees, Essenes, and followers of Yeshua, were not convinced, which tells us that the vast majority of Jewish people did not agree with the Pharisees' oral tradition.[14] We'll take a look at their arguments for the oral Torah, but first we need to know more about what it is.

Let's try to nail down what the oral Torah is. It can get confusing. First, rabbis call it the oral Torah because they claim God gave it to Moses along with the written Torah, but it wasn't supposed to be written down (Shemot Rabbah 47.1). They claim it was supposed to be taught orally from generation to generation, never to be written down—though in the second century CE, they did write it down.[15] Well, they started writing it down. But it's an evolving Torah that is still being written down today and changes with each generation.[16]

The rabbis started to write it down in a book called the Mishnah, which contains the laws. Next, they wrote down commentaries on these laws, called the Gemara. The Mishnah and the Gemara make up the many volumes of the Talmud.[17] There are actually two different contradicting Talmuds written down around the same time. The first was written in Jerusalem, and the second was written in Babylon. Rabbinic leaders decided that the Babylonian Talmud was more accurate than the other, so that's the one that they accepted.[18]

All of the oral Torah is composed of *Halacha* and *Aggadah*. The parts that explain how to live are called Halacha (literally, law). When it is a story, or non-Halacha, it is called Aggadah.[19] The Talmud is composed of the Mishnah and the Gemara[20]—that is, the laws and the commentary.[21] But the oral Torah doesn't stop with the Talmud. Many more books have been written by various sages and rabbis over the past two millennia, adding to the library. So, we have the Shulchan Aruch, the Tur, Chafetz Chaim, Mishnah Brurah, Mishnah Torah, Zohar, and countless more. Even the response of a rabbi to a student's question at a local Yeshiva is considered authoritative oral Torah.

> "When God revealed Himself at Sinai to give the Torah to Israel, He taught to Moses the following order: Bible, Mishnah, Talmud, and Aggadah, as it says: 'God taught all these words, saying', even what a student will ask his teacher. God then said to Moses, after he had learnt it from the mouth of God, "Teach it to Israel'" (Shemot Rabbah 47:1)

We know that the Torah, the written contract, limits the phrase "all the words commanded Moses" to all the words commanded in the book: **"Moses wrote down all the words of YHWH"** (Ex. 24:4). But the rabbis claim that anything they write or even say is the authoritative word of God that he already gave to Moses. This passage in the oral Torah that was written in the early Middle Ages claims that God said the following:

> "I will give them the Bible written, the Mishna, Talmud and Aggada orally. 'Inscribe those words for yourself' 'Inscribe' refers to the Bible, 'for according to those words' refer to the Mishna and Talmud." (Shemot Rabbah 47:1)

This teaching from the Talmud shows that rabbis claim anything they write or say is the authoritative word of God. They try to make room for this claim in the written contract by distorting the clear meaning of the written text. When the written text says **"according to those words,"** they say that means the oral Torah. The problem with their claim is that the biblical text is clear that **"according to those words"** means the written words and leaves no room for words not written down: Exodus 24:7, Deuteronomy 31:9–13, Joshua 8:34–35, 1 Kings 2:2–3, and Proverbs 30:1.

Moses wrote down all the words of YHWH. (Ex. 24:4)

"When all Israel comes to appear before YHWH your God at the place which He will choose, *you shall read this Law* **[Torah] before all Israel so that they hear**

> it. Assemble the people, the men, the women, the children, and the stranger who is in your town, *so that they may* hear and learn and fear YHWH your God, and be careful to follow all the words of this Law." (Deut. 31:11–12)

> "Afterward he read all the words of the Law [Torah]." (Josh. 8:34)

Rabbinic Judaism has taken the authority to add to the words of God by claiming that God taught them everything they are adding. But the book of Proverbs in the Writing section of the Tanakh explains why it's so important not to add to God's words in the Torah or anywhere else:

> Every word of God is pure;
> He is a shield to those who take refuge in Him.
> Do not add to His words
> Or He will rebuke you, and you will be proved a liar.
>
> (Proverbs 30:5–6)

If you're wondering, "Okay, why has God allowed this oral fabrication to continue so long if Proverbs said God 'will rebuke you, and you will be proved a liar' for changing his words?" that is a natural question. Hang on to it for now. Chapter 4 will address it.

The extent of the rabbis' power grab is evident in the Talmudic story "The Oven of Akhnai." This story records an argument between Rabbi Eliezer and Rabbi Yehuda. Eliezer proved Yehuda and the majority wrong, and God himself agreed with Eliezer. God showed that he agreed with Eliezer through a series of miracles, to which the rabbis shockingly responded by saying, essentially, "God, we don't care what you think. We're in charge now." The atrocity in this story speaks for itself.

> Eliezer then said to them: If the *halakha* (oral law) is in accordance with my opinion, Heaven will prove it.

A Divine Voice emerged from Heaven and said: Why are you differing with Rabbi Eliezer, as the *halakha* is in accordance with his opinion in every place that he expresses an opinion? Rabbi Yehoshua stood on his feet and said: It is written: "It is not in heaven" (Deuteronomy 30:12). The Gemara asks: What is the relevance of the phrase "It is not in heaven" in this context? Rabbi Yirmeya says: Since the Torah was already given at Mount Sinai, we do not regard a Divine Voice, as You already wrote at Mount Sinai, in the Torah: "After a majority to incline" (Exodus 23:2). Since the majority of Rabbis disagreed with Rabbi Eliezer's opinion, the *halakha* is not ruled in accordance with his opinion. The Gemara relates: Years after, Rabbi Natan encountered Elijah the prophet and said to him: What did the Holy One, Blessed be He, do at that time, when Rabbi Yehoshua issued his declaration? Elijah said to him: The Holy One, Blessed be He, smiled and said: My children have triumphed over Me; My children have triumphed over Me." (Bava Metzia 59b)

This story in the Talmud tries to prove that rabbis have more authority than God over the Jewish people and the Torah. They even claim God was happy about it. They argue this by clearly twisting two Torah verses. The first verse they misinterpret is Deuteronomy 30:12. If you read the three preceding verses, you'll see that it is actually yet again proving the opposite; it proves that all of the Torah was written down under the authority of God.

> **"YHWH will rejoice over you again for good . . . if you obey YHWH your God, to keep His commandments and His statutes which are written in this Book of the Law, if you turn to YHWH your God with all your heart and soul.**
>
> **"For this commandment which I am commanding you today is not too difficult for you, nor is it far away.**

> It is not in heaven, that you could say, 'Who will go up to heaven for us and get it for us, and proclaim it to us, so that we may follow it?' Nor is it beyond the sea, that you could say, 'Who will cross the sea for us and get it for us and proclaim it to us, so that we may follow it?' On the contrary, the word is very near you, in your mouth and in your heart, that you may follow it." (Deut. 30:9–12)

When you read the textual context of verse 12, you'll see it has nothing to do with God turning over his authority to the sages. It is showing that God gave all his commandments in written form. He tells the people that it's not too difficult because they have it already written down and readily available. The second verse this story used to distort and try to take authority from God is even more egregious: **"You shall not follow the crowd in doing evil, nor shall you testify in a dispute so as to join together with a crowd in order to pervert justice"** (Ex. 23:2).

This verse says, **"You shall not follow the crowd in doing evil."** It suited the rabbis' agenda to follow the crowd, so they removed the word *not* and took the verse completely out of context. They further use this story to claim that as long as there is a majority ruling among the rabbis on any topic, the Jewish people must accept it undisputedly. It is heinously obvious how the sages ripped this verse out of context to make it say what they wanted it to.

Rabbinic Judaism Today Is Nothing More than the Oral Tradition of the Pharisees

Okay, so we've already covered a lot of ground. We've established that the written Torah claims to have at least two purposes: First, to record actual events so that the Jewish people won't forget what God did for them. Second, to serve as the one and only contract between God and the Jewish people until the promised new covenant.

Then we established that a small Jewish group around 150 BCE gained enough political power to introduce and begin to implement a new supposed contract. What was so radical about their new contract is that they claimed God gave it to Moses along with the first one, even though none of the other Jewish people (the vast majority) at the time had even heard of it.

The natural question is, What does the validity of this new oral Torah have to do with being Jewish today? It has to do with understanding Jewish identity today because Judaism today is rabbinical Judaism. Which means Judaism, whether orthodox, conservative, or reform, is nothing more than the oral traditions of the Pharisees.

The renowned Rabbi David Rosen, who was Chief Rabbi of Ireland, summarized well that Judaism today is descended from the Pharisees' oral Torah:

> The bottom line is that Jewish tradition for most of the last two thousand years viewed the Pharisees as the rabbis of our heritage, heirs of the prophets and biblical tradition, the teachers of authentic Judaism as enshrined in the Talmud—as it has been practiced and known until modern times.[22]

Or take it from Professor Avigdor Shinan. He teaches at the Hebrew University of Jerusalem and is considered one of the greatest experts in the sages' literature. Here is what he says, and I couldn't say it better:

> Our theology is not the theology of the OT. The tradition that we follow today is not the tradition of the OT. It's the tradition of the Sages. Shabbat laws, kashrut laws, you name it, it's not in the Scriptures, not in the OT. In the OT, there is no synagogue, no Kaddish, no Kol Nidre, no bar mitzvah, no tallit. Everything that somebody would define as Jewish and look for its root . . . it's not the OT. It's the Sages' literature. That's where everything started.[23]

The traditions of Judaism today, from bar mitzvahs and kippahs to the kashrut laws, none of it appears in the Torah. It all started with the Pharisees asserting their traditions as law. Israeli scholar Eitan Bar explains that these traditions are not only absent from the contract between God and the Jewish people, but they are actually a result of cultural diffusion with other ancient cultures.

> Most of Jewish traditions have even been taken from other peoples, among whom our people lived during times of exile: Talismans, the Hamsa (hand-shaped charms), Lag b'Omer, wearing of a kippah/yarmulke, seances, wrapping of tefillin, mezuzahs, lying prostrate on the graves of the famous rabbis, the kashrut laws of separating meat and dairy, magic, Bar Mitzvahs, displaying pictures of famous rabbis, saying mantras and even the tradition of breaking of a wine glass at weddings.
>
> All these beloved traditions are not mentioned once in the Bible. You might wonder now: But wait, doesn't the Torah mention the tefillin and the mezuzah? Not really. The sages chose one or two words from a verse taken out of its context and by force gave it a new meaning.[24]

The verse Bar is referring to that was taken out of context to prove the necessity of tefillin and mezuzah are from the Shema. The sages ignore the clearly symbolic message of the passage, which is that the Torah should be cherished and used to guide every area of a Jewish person's life, and they instead manipulated it in an attempt to prescribe wrapping tefillin around your arm and putting a mezuzah on your door.

> **"Hear, Israel, YHWH is our God, YHWH is one. And you shall love YHWH your God with all your heart and with all your soul and with all your strength. These words, which I am commanding you today, shall be on your heart. And you shall repeat them diligently to your sons and speak of them when you sit in your**

house, when you walk down the road, when you lie down, and when you get up. You shall also tie them as a sign to your hand, and they shall be as frontlets [totafot] on your forehead. You shall also write them on the doorposts of your house and on your gates." (Deut. 6:4–9)

There is some debate among Hebrew scholars on whether the word translated here as **"frontlets"** (*totafot* in Hebrew), comes from the word root *netifot*, meaning "hanging," or from the word root *tafa*, meaning "encircle."[25] Either way, the message is the same: A person's focus should be on the words of God. The sages took this debate as an opportunity to assert the necessity of the oral Torah (Sanhedrin 88b). They claim that because we don't know if the Hebrew word means "encircle" or "hanging" (between our eyes), we can't know how to put totafot on correctly without the oral Torah to tell us how. In other words, they say the Torah just tells us to put on totafot; it doesn't tell us enough to know how to do that. In other words, the Talmud is declaring that this verse is not about authentic devotion to God but is actually commanding that we need to put on a physical thing known as tefillin and to put up a physical thing called a mezuzah on our door (Talmud Sanhedrin 4b).

But the passage is clearly not a physical command, because it starts out by saying, **"These words shall be upon your heart"** (Deut. 6:6), and I don't know anyone who has had open-heart surgery to keep the Shema.

Man wearing tefellin

God told the prophet Isaiah what he desires for his people: that they genuinely trust him, not try to earn his favor with man-made religion.

> **"I will look to this one,**
> **At one who is humble and contrite in spirit, and who trembles at My word."**
>
> (Isa. 66:2)

God also told Isaiah that people would try to approach him with these empty religious traditions anyway instead of sincerely seeking him with their hearts.

> **"...This people approaches Me with their words**
> **And honors Me with their lips,**
> **But their heart is far away from Me,**
> **And their reverence for Me consists of the commandment of men that is taught."**
>
> (Isa. 29:13)

The God of the Hebrew Bible doesn't support man-made religious institutions or rules. Those only make the people who follow them dependent on the human teacher instead of God. If a teacher convinces you that if you don't have a mezuzah on your door, you are disobeying the Creator of the universe, then you have become dependent on that teacher instead of God. Because now the teacher is the only one with the authority to tell you what goes inside the mezuzah, or how to angle it on your door, and so on.

Without these extra laws that are not in the Torah, there would be no reason to have an oral Law. If you add extra laws and tell the people they're getting only some of the laws in the written Torah, suddenly you've become necessary to the people, because they can only get the supposedly missing laws from you. Adopting traditions from nearby cultures and passing them off as God's commands was the Pharisees' way to take power.

From a modern perspective, it seems impossible that a change like this could have happened without an entire nation of people realizing they were being duped. But in light of some profound and straightforward facts about the Jewish people during this time, it eerily starts to make much more sense. Remember, as the Pharisees aligned themselves with Queen Alexandra, they acquired so much power they could arrest or free anyone they chose. At least some of the priests were afraid of the Pharisees. Even though the Pharisees were a small group, it would be hard not to fear them, and they were actively opposing the priesthood. The Pharisees gained ground aggressively in this power struggle.

With the priests already backing down to the Pharisees as religious leaders, when the temple was destroyed in 70 CE, the priests' authority disappeared. It was tied to the temple, and when the temple was destroyed, the Pharisees easily took any authority the priests had left.

Let's not forget how the everyday Jewish person was learning Torah. We're talking about a pre-Gutenberg civilization. Each scroll had to be copied by hand. These were expensive and not available in every house. The scrolls of Scripture were only owned by synagogues or, occasionally, a very wealthy person. Learning Torah required a person to go to the synagogue, where it would be read to them. Very

Origins of Rabbinic Judaism

likely, a Pharisee would often be the one who would read it. Even when it wasn't a Pharisee, it's evident that the Pharisees were imposing their teachings on others, even the priests, to the point of stoning. When the Pharisees read you the written Torah, they would primarily slip in the oral Torah. How would you know when one started and the other began if it was being read to you?

And this was *before* the fall of the temple in 70 CE. Afterward, the Pharisees actually began to censor the Torah.[26] According to the same practice, when rabbis translate the Torah today, they do so in accordance with teachings from the oral Torah. That means the Torah no longer conveys the text's original message, because if the meaning conflicts with the oral Torah, which it often does, the rabbinic editors just change it. They change it to justify the oral Law's influence on the Jewish people— and by extension the Rabbis influence on the Jewish people.

Today if you learn Torah with a Rabbi, more than likely you won't even be learning from one of these altered Torahs. You'll most likely read from something labeled "Torah" or "The Five Books of Moses." But it won't be the true Torah. You'll read from a Torah with words from the rabbis' teaching actually inserted right in the middle of the sentences. Usually, these inserted words completely change the meaning of the sentence. As you can imagine, you can make anything say anything you want if you just put your own words in the middle.

Let's take a sentence from the Torah and then see the same sentence in one of the altered Torahs that rabbis encourage you to use. Remember, these books are usually just labeled "Torah" or "The Five Books of Moses," so you wouldn't necessarily know there was oral Torah stuffed inside. In the following example, I'll use the rabbis' translation, but I'll take out the inserted words the first time.

> *Original:* **God said, "Let Us make man in our mold, like Us, and let him rule over the fish of the sea, over the birds of the skies, over the cattle, over all the earth and over all the creeping things that creep upon the earth!"** (Gen. 1:26)

> *Stuffed:* God (consulted the heavenly court and) said, "Let Us make man in our mold (intellectually endowed), like Us, and (if he is worthy) let him rule over the fish of the sea, over the birds of the skies, over the cattle, over all the earth and over all the creeping things that creep upon the earth!"[27]

As you can see, by inserting these words, the rabbinic editors take the meaning of the text and hold it hostage to whatever they want it to say. God says, **"Let him rule over all the earth."** But the rabbis decided God only meant man to rule if he was worthy. Is it possible that God only meant the human to rule if he was worthy? Yes; however, that is not what the text says, so it is not an accurate translation of the text. This stuffed Torah is nothing more than a commentary disguised as an undistorted original.

The sages did more than create a new Torah; they claim the authority to translate the original Torah and insert words from their creation into the original. Moreover, they heavily discourage Jewish people from studying the Torah and instead push them to spend their time studying the Talmud.

The Talmud says the following:

> For those who engage in the study of Bible, it is a virtue but not a complete virtue. For those who engage in the study of Mishna, it is a virtue and they receive reward for its study. For those who engage in the study of Talmud, you have no virtue greater than that. (Bava Metzia 33a)

In other words, studying the Bible is fine, but really you should study the Talmud because there is nothing better than studying Talmud. Rashi, one of the most recognized sages in Judaism, added this: "Do not let them get used to learning the Bible." And Maimonides explained that one should not learn anything except for Talmud: "He should focus his attention on the *Gemara* alone for his entire life" (Hilchos Talmud Torah: Chapter 1:12).

The Oral Torah in Orthodox, Conservative, and Reform Traditions

Reform

Today the main rabbinic Jewish denominations are Orthodox, Conservative, and Reform. These three main denominations didn't appear until the nineteenth century. Before then, rabbinic Judaism took the form only of what would today be considered Orthodox Judaism.[28] Different traditions were based on location and cultural implementation, but they still fell under orthodoxy.

The place of the oral Torah in Orthodox Judaism is made evident by the statements of famed rabbis such as Maimonides and in the Talmud itself. The question is, do the Conservative and Reform movements also revolve around the teachings of the oral Torah instead of the Tanakh?

To understand the place of the oral Torah in the Reform and Conservative Jewish identities, I think it's helpful to understand the origins of these movements. These movements are both very new relative to the origins of the Jewish people and even to rabbinic Judaism. Reform Judaism began in Germany in the early 1800s as an attempt to assimilate with society without abandoning Jewish identity.[29] The movement began in Germany, but it flourished in the United States. The United States, known as the world's melting pot, was the perfect environment to promote the watering down of traditional rabbinic Judaism. The goal of Reform Judaism, then, was simply to take the inconvenience out of Judaism.[30]

Nearly all of the traditions people associate with Jewishness today are present in Reform Judaism: bar mitzvahs, Rosh Hashana, breaking a glass at a wedding, and so on. And all of these come from the oral Torah. Reform Judaism is not a Judaism that disconnects from the oral Torah. While the Reform tradition doesn't consider studying the oral Torah as important as adherents of Orthodox Judaism do, they still consider it "The Form and Substance of Jewish Law."[31] It makes sense: Reform Judaism is an attempt to make Judaism more convenient while still maintaining the identity defined in the Talmud, whereas Orthodox Judaism sees studying the Talmud as the most essential thing in life (Bavia Metzia 33a). In an attempt to conform with local norms, Reform Judaism doesn't require obedience to all the laws in the Talmud or the Torah, but it still roots its identity in the Talmud, the same as Orthodoxy.

Reform Judaism teaches that all of the Torah and oral Torah teachings are good and true, but not all the commands are necessarily required. They only require obedience to ethical laws, claiming that the rest are up to the individual.[32] However, according to the Torah, a Jew must obey all the commands with no exceptions. After giving the Torah to Israel, God through Moses told the people that if they obeyed all the laws, he would bless them. Then he listed several blessings they would receive upon the specific condition that they keep all of the laws. Moses opened by emphasizing that the people needed to keep all of the laws.

The passage begins:

> **"Now it shall be, if you diligently obey YHWH your God, being careful to do all His commandments which I am commanding you today, that YHWH your God will put you high above all the nations of the earth."** (Deut. 28:1)

Then Moses listed several blessings and closed the blessing section the same way he opened it, by stipulating that the blessings would only apply if the people obeyed all of the commandments and not disobey any of them.

> **"YHWH will make you the head and not the tail, and you will only be above, and not be underneath, if you listen to the commandments of YHWH your God which I am commanding you today, to follow them carefully, and do not turn aside from any of the words which I am commanding you today, to the right or the left, to pursue other gods to serve them."** (vv. 13–14)

As if it wasn't emphasized enough, immediately following this, God told the people what would happen if they disobeyed any of these laws. Many curses would come upon them. To God, obeying every one of the commands was important and central to the Torah's teaching. This makes sense. These laws were given to govern the Nation of Israel. You don't get to pick and choose which national laws to follow.

Imagine someone sitting on trial for murder: "Your honor, yes, I murdered that person, but I've kept most of the other laws, so I'm not guilty." Ridiculous. It only takes breaking one law to be a criminal. You can't separate the teachings of the Torah from the commands of the Torah. If the God of the Torah is real, and if his instructions in the Torah are good, then he rightfully expects full obedience.

> **"But it shall come about, if you do not obey YHWH your God, to be careful to follow all His commandments and His statutes which I am commanding you today, that all these curses will come upon you and overtake you."** (v. 15)

God opened the curses section by again emphasizing the importance of obeying every law. Then he lists curse after curse that would come about if the people didn't obey all these laws.

I once listened to this section on an audio recording. It took about five minutes to get through the curses. According to the Torah, after the people agreed to the covenant, God had Moses read this whole passage to the people at once. As an Israelite, listening to all of the things God would do for you if you obeyed all the laws would undoubtedly impress on you how important each law was to God. Especially when he followed it by an even longer reading, for several minutes, of the curses you'd receive if you didn't follow all of them. God ended the curse section with the same emphasis:

> **"If you are not careful to follow all the words of this Law that are written in this book, to fear this honored and awesome name, YHWH your God, then YHWH will bring extraordinary plagues on you and your**

descendants, severe and lasting plagues, and miserable and chronic sicknesses." (vv. 58–59)

You can't strip the laws from the teachings of the Torah. They are one and the same. Yet, that's exactly what reform Judaism does. All that Reform Judaism leaves of the Jewish identity are the traditions that the Pharisees and rabbis created with the oral Torah. So, this branch is even further separated from the Judaism of the Tanakh.

Conservative

Scholars suggest that Conservative Judaism was an inevitable byproduct of Reform Judaism. Reform Judaism was a dilution of rabbinic Judaism, so the Orthodox label was intended as a counter-reformation.[33] Essentially, these two denominations of Judaism were on the opposite sides of the rabbinic spectrum, naturally leaving people in the middle. The people in the middle became known as Conservatives.

As you'd expect, the Talmud is central to Conservative Judaism, just like it is to the Orthodox and Reform communities. Conservative rabbi Ismar Schorsch, who was chancellor emeritus of the Jewish Theological Seminary, explained the importance of the Talmud in his book about the seven core values of Conservative Judaism. He lists the conservative values in the following order: "God, Torah, Talmud Torah, Halakhah, the Land and State of Israel, Klal Yisrael and Hebrew."[34] Don't be fooled by how Talmud and Halakhah appear after Torah on that list; remember that the Talmud explains how to follow the written Torah. So even if you are reading the Torah as well as the Talmud, the Talmud will change the meaning of the Torah by necessity.

There are many unique differences between the three denominations in interpreting and applying the oral and written Torahs. But all three groups hold to the oral Torah, and their disagreements all come from how to interpret and follow it.

Rabbis might try to argue otherwise, but it is clear that the Talmud is the central text of all rabbinical Judaism, whether Orthodox,

Conservative, or Reform. Remember, all of the traditions that people associate with Jewishness today come from the Talmud, from bar mitzvahs to Rosh Hashana. (Rosh Hashana is not in the Bible; it replaces the biblical feast of trumpets, which has nothing to do with a new year. In fact, the Torah says that Passover is the new year; see Leviticus 23:5.) The main problem with Talmud being the central text is that the Torah is supposed to be the central text of Judaism. The Talmud claims that it gets its validity and authority from the Torah. But as we've already seen, the Torah leaves no room for an additional Torah.

Imagine that in the United States a new political party starts to gain massive political power. This new political party passes a law that says soldiers can force themselves into your house and live there if they need to. Every other US party would be outraged. How can you pass that law? It directly contradicts the Third Amendment! But the new party leaders answer: Yes, but the oral Constitution gives us more information that allows soldiers to take up residence if they have enough need. This would obviously be absurd. And it would be even more outrageous if the first written contract, which is still in force, explicitly states that nothing can be added to it during its life.

This shows how ridiculous the idea of the oral Torah is. Writing down a contract ensures that all of the terms of your agreement are documented to avoid future manipulation. Yet manipulation of the agreement is exactly what the oral Torah does. The Torah was a constitution of sorts between Israel and their God that laid out all the laws and said not to add new laws. Then the Pharisees gained enough political power to add new laws, which they slipped in through their oral constitution.

If we want to embrace our Jewish identity, there is a choice presented to us. We can choose to follow the rabbinic version of Judaism, which is inconsistent because, while it claims to follow the Torah, it instead follows the Oral Law. Or we can follow the Torah that was given on Mount Sinai.

If you adhere to rabbinical Judaism even culturally, you mustn't fool yourself into thinking you are following God or even following the Judaism of our ancestors. The traditions and laws a rabbinical Jew follows—whether they are Orthodox, Conservative or Reform—are nothing more than traditions created by a group of people. A group of people who managed to gain political power and use it to become the lawgivers of the Jewish people in place of God. This is a very bold claim, so let's examine some more evidence.

Chapter 2: Summary

Part 1: Rise of the Pharisees and the birth of the oral Torah.

1. Around 150 BCE a Jewish sect formed and introduced, for the first time, an oral tradition that they claimed was given to Moses along with the Torah.
2. All of the other Jewish sects rejected that idea and claimed the oral Torah was not given to Moses.
3. The Pharisees gained tremendous political power by aligning themselves with Queen Alexandra.
4. They used their power to scare the priests into submission and assume authority over the lives of the Jewish people.
5. They tried to justify their power by altering the meanings of texts through translation, inserting their own words into the text without notice, and simply twisting the meaning of the Torah.
6. After the temple fell, they were able to convince the Jewish nation of their authority because the common Israelite didn't have access to Torah scrolls. The Torah would nearly always be read to them.

Part 2: What the majority of people today think is Judaism, is *not*. It's just the Pharisees' traditions.

1. Even renowned Jewish scholars admit that nothing people associate with Jewishness today comes from the Torah (e.g., Professor Avigdor Shinan). Yet the same Torah demands to be the center of Jewish life.
2. After wedging their own authority into the teachings of the Torah, the rabbis actually steered people away from the Torah and taught them to study only the oral Torah. (Bava Metzia 33a)

Conclusion: The oral Torah is a later addition to a written contract that explicitly states, multiple times, that no additions are to be accepted. This later, illegitimate addition then replaced the original to such an extent that people associate Judaism with the counterfeit addition instead of the original.

3

THE ORAL TORAH EXAMINED

Now that we've discussed the origins of the oral Law and its direct connection to rabbinic Judaism, this needs to be clearly stated. The traditions themselves are not the problem, in fact, many of the traditions are valuable and rich. These traditions in the Mishneh and Talmud, have played a major role in preserving our people through the past two thousand years of diaspora. I have great respect for our traditions and for Rabbis. Most rabbis are very sincere. The problem is that in rabbinic Judaism, these traditions have functionally replaced the Tanakh.

If we want to embrace our Jewish identity, we have in front of us two paths. The teaching of the Torah, or the teaching of the oral Torah. The oral Torah would have us believe that it is not only compatible with the written Torah, but that it is actually rooted in the written Torah. This chapter will show that these two bodies of law are contradictory and incompatible.

By now, there are a few things about the Torah and oral Torah that should be clear. First, the Torah claims that it is the central text of the Jewish people. Even King David saw the Torah as the main text;

his dying command to his son was to study the written Torah. Rabbis teach that the Torah is truth but that the Talmud should be the central text. But, the Torah can't be the authentic word of God and not be the main text. If the Torah is true then it has to be the central text (1 Kings 2:2, Joshua 1:8, Psalm 1). The sages justified the need for the Talmud by taking key verses and twisting them: **"Do not follow a multitude," "frontlets between your eyes,"** etc.... These alterations show that the sages weren't motivated by proper interpretation, but by power. Now we'll take a look at some more key ways that the oral Law is not compatible with the Hebrew Bible.

Oral Torah's Incompatibility with the Narrative of the Hebrew Bible

By now we know that the written Torah makes it clear there can be no oral Torah. Furthermore, an oral Torah is never mentioned in any of the three collections that make up the Tanakh. If there was an oral contract that accompanied the written contract, then the history of the Jewish people—from Abraham through the First Temple and its destruction, all the way through the Second Temple period recorded in the Hebrew Bible—would have had to mention it at least once. But no mention appears in the Tanakh.

No biblical figure ever discusses the oral Torah.

No biblical figure is ever described as following the oral Torah, teaching it, studying it, quoting from it, or interacting with it at all.

And most importantly, there is no biblical evidence or other evidence that anyone was ever sentenced by its rules until the Pharisees.

The rabbinic claim is that God gave the oral Torah to Moses at Mt. Sinai. This is recorded in the oral Torah itself:

> When God revealed Himself at Sinai to give the Torah to Israel, He taught to Moses the following order: Bible, Mishnah, Talmud, and Aggadah, as it says: "God taught all these words, saying," even what a student will ask his teacher. God then said to Moses, after he had learnt

it from the mouth of God, "Teach it to Israel." (Shemot Rabbah 47:1.)

However, the Hebrew Bible shows there were several times where Moses would have used an oral Torah if he had one. But he didn't know what to do, so he had to ask God. For instance, God had given Moses the Passover commands at Mt. Sinai, some men were confused about how they should follow one of the rules, so naturally, they went and asked Moses what they should do. Moses didn't know the answer, so he asked God: **"Moses then said to them, 'Wait, and I will listen to what YHWH will command concerning you'"** (Num. 9:8). Leviticus 24, Numbers 15, and Numbers 27 all contain more examples of Moses consulting God because he didn't know how to carry out one of God's commands. Since the oral Torah is supposed to answer all such questions, but Moses didn't know how to answer them, he couldn't have had the oral Torah.

Rabbinical Judaism claims that the oral Torah was studied and followed even before Moses (Mishnah Kiddushin 4). They claim Adam, Abraham, Jacob, and others studied it, but in the Tanakh, none of them are ever shown obeying it. Some important biblical figures are shown acting in ways that would be disobedient to it, and of God approving their actions.

There are kosher laws in the Tanakh, but they are different from the kosher laws of the oral Torah. One of the more obvious departures from the biblical commands in rabbinical Judaism is an added prohibition against eating meat and cheese together.[1] You can see the justification for this addition if you look at Rashi's commentary on Exodus 34:26. This prohibition is a well-known kosher law among observant rabbinic Jews. I encourage you to read Genesis 18. The story is too long to quote in its entirety here, so we'll get right to it.

One day, YHWH and some angels visited Abraham, so Abraham prepared them a meal. **"He took curds and milk and the calf which he had prepared, and set it before them; and he was standing by them under the tree as they ate"** (Gen. 18:8). So Abraham served God meat, milk, and cheese. Abraham's actions would violate the oral

Torah's kosher laws—the same oral Torah laws Abraham supposedly practiced. Yet YHWH doesn't rebuke Abraham for breaking the oral Torah; instead, he eats with Abraham. If eating meat and dairy really was prohibited, God wouldn't eat meat and dairy with Abraham.

In 2 Samuel 17:29, the same thing happens again. This time it is King David—the same King David who supposedly followed the commands of the oral Torah—who plainly violates them, just like Abraham, by eating cheese and meat together and giving it to all the hungry people.

If the commands in the oral Torah were from the biblical God, then the Bible wouldn't show biblical figures breaking the oral Torah as no big deal, and it certainly wouldn't show God participating in breaking his own law.

Different Gods in the Torah and Oral Torah: Women, Gentiles, Magic, and Honesty

The inconsistencies between the oral Torah and Hebrew Bible aren't just present in the terms of the contractual relationship and the laws. There are also decisive differences in the character of God in the oral and written Torah's. If these are both accurate descriptions of the same God, then his character should be consistent between them, yet we'll see that they are not. Specifically, the way God feels about women, gentiles and honesty is entirely different in the oral and written Torahs.

God and Women

When the Hebrew Bible introduces the first woman in Genesis 2, God says he created her to be a "helper" suitable for Adam. **"Then YHWH God said, 'It is not good for the man to be alone; I will make him a helper suitable for him'"** (Gen. 2:18). Remember, it is Adam's job to rule over the earth, so the woman is created to help him rule over the earth. She's supposed to be a coruler. The Hebrew word translated here as **"helper"** is *ezer*. It would be a mistake to think that her position as a helper is inferior to Adam. The same word, *ezer*, is used over and over again to describe God helping humans. Clearly, in the Tanakh, neither God nor the biblical authors see humans as superior to God. Furthermore, just a little later, God says that when a man is joined to his wife, **"they shall become one flesh"** (Gen. 2:24). The picture then of men and women is one of equal value. Men and women were intended to be royal leaders on the earth, each made in the image of God. **"So God created man in His own image, in the image of God he created him; male and female He created them"** (Gen. 1:27). The word "man" here is not gender-specific and refers to mankind. For this reason, some translations use the word "human."

The point is, men and women are both created in the image of God to rule over the earth as God's representatives. In Genesis 3, when God tells Adam and Eve the consequences of their sin, he says to the woman that her husband will rule over her. We shouldn't mistake this as God's original design or how he views women. He's not commanding the husband to rule over his wife; he's telling Eve that wasn't supposed to happen, but now it is what will happen due to the couple's bringing evil into creation. God wanted them to rule over the earth together, but because they sinned, that won't happen, and the husband will rule over his wife. The God of the Bible does not see women as less important or of less value than men.

Just like God said would happen, there are examples in the Tanakh of men abusing power over women. We read stories of men mistreating, taking advantage of, and even raping women. When God's chosen man, Abraham, didn't have a child in a timeline that made sense to him, he slept with his wife's slave (Gen. 16:1–4). You can decide if that was some form of abuse, but to me, a master sleeping with a slave doesn't sound consensual.

Other times, scared for his life, Abraham lied about who his wife, Sarah, was and let kings take her (Gen. 12:11–19; 20:1–10). Later Isaac would do the same thing to his wife (Gen. 26:6–10). Judah and his sons had a responsibility to Judah's daughter-in-law Tamar, but they neglected and even sexually abused her (Gen. 38:1–26).

King David had a married woman brought to him. He slept with her, then murdered her husband to cover it up (2 Sam. 11). We aren't told if she came willingly or not, but David was king, so she wouldn't have had a choice.

There are many more stories of men abusing power over women in the Tanakh. How do all these stories line up with God's view of women as inherently valuable and loved? They don't. Instead, each time a woman is mistreated in the Tanakh, it is depicted as evil. Even if the story doesn't blatantly state that what happened was evil to God (as in 2 Sam. 11:27), it shows how what happened was wrong. Moreover, God personally appeared to Hagar and promised to care for her (Gen. 16: 9-13), and he protected Sarah and Rebekah when their husbands handed them over to the kings of Egypt and Gerar (Gen. 12:17-18; 20:3-7; 26:8-11). The God of the Torah loves women and condemns their abuse.

But the God described in the oral Torah has a different view of women. Mistreating women is not condemned; it's actually approved. The first example is a Gemara story in which the rabbi is explaining why it's foolish for men to chase after women: "A woman is a flask full of feces and her mouth is full of blood" (Tractate Shabbat 152a). The Rambam, Maimonides, one of the most respected rabbis in Judaism, wrote that the man has a right to make his wife do household chores and other similar things for him even by beating her: "Whenever a woman refrains from performing any of the tasks that she is obligated to perform, she may be compelled to do so, even with a rod" (Mishnah Torah Ishut 21:10).

While Maimonides wrote that a man must not have sex with his wife without her consent if she is afraid ("He should not engage in relations with her against her will when she is afraid of him" [Mishnah Torah Issurei Biah 21:12]), he doesn't need her consent if she is not afraid:

> A man's wife is permitted to him. Therefore, a man may do whatever he desires with his wife. He may engage in relations whenever he desires, kiss any organ he desires, engage in vaginal or anal intercourse or engage in physical intimacy without relations. (Mishnah Torah Issurei Biah 21:9)

Today we consider this domestic rape.

The oral Torah does not always speak of women in this condescending way. Sometimes the oral Torah says good things about women. However, these condescending remarks sufficiently show that the God of the oral Torah does not value women as much as men. The Tanakh, on the other hand, shows that God values women and men equally. The way the God depicted in the oral Torah feels about women contrasts directly with the loving way the God of the Torah sees women. They cannot both be an accurate description of the same God.

God and Gentiles

There is a similar contradiction with how the God of the Bible feels about non-Jewish people versus how the God of the oral Torah feels about them.

Remember from earlier that the plot conflict of the Torah begins with two non-Jewish people who bring evil into the world, and God hatches a plan to save humans and creation from the evil now in the world. Later Abraham is chosen as the first step in that plan to deal with the sin problem humans created: **"In you all the families of the earth will be blessed"** (Gen. 12:3). Also, God changes Abram's name to Abraham to signify that Abraham isn't going to be the father of one nation only but that God's purpose is to bless many nations:

> **"No longer shall you be named Abram,**
> **But your name shall be Abraham;**
> **For I have made you the father of a multitude of nations."**
>
> (Gen. 17:5)

The more you read the Abraham story, the more evident it becomes that God is interested in more than just the well-being of Abraham and his descendants, the people of Israel. He care for them precisely because he cares so much about all the world's nations.

The rest of the Hebrew Bible tracks the history of the Jewish people and how they function in God's plan to get rid of the sin problem in the world. But it doesn't exclusively focus on the Jewish people. In the book of Jonah, we see more of God's love for the Gentiles. He sends the Jewish prophet Jonah to go and tell the gentile people of Nineveh that they are living immorally, but that God doesn't want to destroy them. He is patient and wants to forgive them if they will repent and trust his definition of good and evil.

Jonah doesn't want to deliver this message because he hates the Ninevites. He tells God he avoided going to Ninevah because he knew God loved them and would forgive them. **"Therefore in anticipation of this I fled to Tarshish, since I knew that You are a gracious and compassionate God, slow to anger and abundant in mercy, and One who relents of disaster"** (Jonah 4:2). God confirms that Jonah is right about how God feels towards the gentiles: **"Should I not also have compassion on Nineveh, the great city in which there are more than 120,000 people...?"** (Jonah 4:11).

We also talked earlier about how, through the prophet Jeremiah, God promised he would one day introduce a new covenant because Israel didn't keep the laws of the Torah. In the new covenant, there would be no separation between Israel and the rest of humankind anymore. The prophet Hosea also spoke about the same future covenant: **"I will say to those who were not My people, 'You are My people!' And they will say, 'You are my God!'"** (Hosea 2:23).

The God depicted in the oral Torah does not share the same love for gentiles as the God of Abraham, Isaac, and Jacob in the Bible. It actually teaches, in the Shulchan Aruch, that it's forbidden to save a gentile's life unless letting them die would cause people to hate Jews: "One must not heal them, even for payment, unless there is reason to save them on the grounds of preventing hatred of Jews" (*Bet Yosef*, Yoreh Deah 158). Rabbi Yoel Sirkis, a leading commentator, wrote that this means indirectly causing the death of a non-Jew is not even a sin (*Bayit Hadash*, commentary on *Bet Yosef*, Yoreh Deah 158). Already we can see that in the oral Torah, God does not seem to care for the gentiles.

Whereas the narrative in the Tanakh shows that God is using

the Jewish people in his plan to rid the world of the sin problem and restore people from every nation to their intended place, the plan in the oral Torah is much different. In the oral Torah, the Gentiles seem to be much less important to God. Ha'ARI wrote, "The gentiles have neither spirit nor soul and are not even equal to animals considered clean, but rather lower than them." Rabbi Tzadik wrote, "Only Israel is called 'human.' In comparison to Israel, all the gentiles are anyhow like beasts that just look human."

Again, the Hebrew Bible has a very different understanding of gentiles. The written Torah says:

> **"When a stranger resides with you in your land, you shall not do him wrong. The stranger who resides with you shall be to you as the native among you, and you shall love him as yourself, for you were strangers in the land of Egypt; I am YHWH your God."** (Lev. 19:33–34)

As with women, the oral Torah doesn't always speak of gentiles so callously, but the fact that it does speak this way at all about gentiles sufficiently shows that the God of the Bible and the God of the oral Torah cannot both be an accurate description of the same God.

God and Magic

In the Tanakh, God strictly prohibits the practice of magic or sorcery. According to the Tanakh, the nations surrounding the Jewish people practiced many forms of magic. In the Torah, God speaks strongly against magical practices and tells the Jewish people to refrain from all forms of magic. He says these things are evil to him, and the Jewish people are not to be influenced by the people around them into performing magic of any kind.

There are multiple condemnations of magic in the Torah and throughout the Tanakh, including a comprehensive list in Deuteronomy that well shows how God feels about magic:

> **"When you enter the land which YHWH your God is**

> giving you, you shall not learn to imitate the detestable things of those nations. There shall not be found among you anyone who makes his son or his daughter pass through the fire, one who uses divination, a soothsayer, one who interprets omens, or a sorcerer, or one who casts a spell, or a medium, or a spiritist, or one who consults the dead. For whoever does these things is detestable to YHWH; and because of these detestable things YHWH your God is going to drive them out before you." (Deut. 18:9-12)

One might expect that the Tanakh would show that magic is ineffective or not real. Instead, God uses magic as an opportunity to show that he is more powerful. When he used Moses and Aaron to bring the Israelites out of Egypt, he sent them to Pharaoh as his representatives. He wanted the Egyptians to know he is God. His first step was to show that Pharaoh's magicians were powerless compared to him. God told Moses that Pharaoh would test him by telling him to perform a miracle. He told Moses to have Aaron throw his staff down on the ground when that time came.

> So Moses and Aaron came to Pharaoh, and so they did, just as YHWH had commanded; and Aaron threw his staff down before Pharaoh and his servants, and it turned into a serpent. Then Pharaoh also called for the wise men and the sorcerers, and they too, the soothsayer priests of Egypt, did the same with their secret arts. For each one threw down his staff, and they turned into serpents. But Aaron's staff swallowed their staffs. Yet Pharaoh's heart was hardened, and he did not listen to them, just as YHWH had said (Ex. 7:10-13).

You can see that Moses and Aaron weren't practicing magic. They were obeying God, and God showed he was more powerful than the magicians who were practicing "secret arts." Aaron's staff swallowed up the magician's staffs, displaying God's dominance over them.

There are other similar stories in which God uses one of his people to show he is more powerful than magicians. One such story involves the prophet Daniel while he was in captivity in Babylon. The king watched Daniel and his three Israelite friends grow up. He noted that they were wiser and smarter than all the magicians and conjurers, groups ancient cultures typically viewed as wise. (See Dan. 1:20).

Contrary to God's warning and command, the Jewish people did end up becoming influenced by these other nations over time, as evidenced by the approval and teaching of magic in the oral Torah. On one hand, the oral Torah acknowledges the prohibition against magic. But because it also teaches and allows for magic, it justifies the magic by sweeping it under the rug and claiming that magic performed by rabbis is in the power of the Torah, so it's okay. That argument doesn't hold water since God commanded that there would be *no* magic. He gave a comprehensive list prohibiting *anyone* who, among other things, "**casts a spell**" (Deut. 18:11). He doesn't qualify that command by saying no one can cast a spell if they do it in the power of a demon. To the God of the Bible, magic is magic, and spells are spells. If anyone casts a spell, it is not by God's power. Nevertheless, the Talmud approves of the use of certain rabbinic magic.

> Abaye says: The halakhot of sorcery are like the halakhot of Shabbat, in that their actions can be divided into three categories: There are some of them for which one is liable to be executed by stoning, and there are some of them for which one is exempt from punishment by Torah law, but they are prohibited by rabbinic law, and there are some of them that are permitted ab initio. (Sanhedrin 67b)

I want to be clear that rabbis don't teach that anyone can practice magic or that it is entirely okay. But the oral Torah does allow for it under certain conditions, so it is not considered inherently forbidden. The use of magic in Judaism is referred to as Kabbalah Massait and is only acceptable for the most righteous individuals.[2] Kabbalah Massait is known as white magic, which, to make a complex definition too simple, means using magic for good instead of bad.[3] Magic in the oral Torah is only considered appropriate on rare occasions and by qualified people. Studying magic within rabbinic Judaism is a highly exclusive practice, but it is not forbidden.

The written Torah, however, categorically forbids any practice of magic. The two Torahs cannot have been given by the same God. Their laws are not compatible with each other.

God and the Truth

"You shall not give false testimony against your neighbor" (Ex. 20:16). Throughout the Tanakh, the trustworthiness of God is an essential theme. The truth is so important to God that his command to be honest appears in the Ten Commandments. God demands honesty throughout the Tanakh; in the Ten Commandments it is specifically a matter of bearing witness accurately. The Hebrew/biblical word for giving testimony or bearing witness is *ed*. Just as with the English word *witness*, this word has a passive function and an active function. To bear witness, or share your experience of an event, you first need to witness the event or experience it. So when God forbids giving false testimony, he's saying, "After you've experienced or witnessed an event, do not lie about it." Being an accurate witness is vital to the God described in the Hebrew Bible.

Along with the honesty of God's people, the Hebrew Bible is concerned with God's own thoroughly honest character. The biblical authors seem to think it is a crucial aspect of his being. God expects people to trust him unwaveringly. In fact, that's how the sin problem got started in the first place. Adam and Eve did not trust that what God had told them about good and evil was true, so they believed the deceiver instead. God took that seriously, the punishment of sin being death, leading to a separation between God and people (Is. 59:2; Ezek. 18:4).

In Genesis 15, God made Abraham a promise, and Abraham believed God. Just like God took the unbelief of Adam and Eve seriously, he took Abraham's belief seriously: **"Then [Abraham]**

believed in YHWH; and He credited it to him as righteousness" (Genesis 15:6). God counted Abraham righteous, or in good standing with him, not because of anything Abraham did, but just because he believed God was trustworthy.

It is essential to the biblical authors that God is fully honest—that he does not lie, and all his words are pure and true:

> **The sum of Your word is truth,**
> **And every one of Your righteous judgements is everlasting.**
>
> (Ps. 119:160)

> **Every word of God is pure;**
> **He is a shield to those who take refuge in Him**
>
> (Proverbs 30:5)

> **God is not a man, that He would lie.**
>
> (Numbers 23:19)

God's completely honest nature is why he is so concerned with the honesty of his people. Because God is good, his expectations for his people are a spilling over of his own good character.

However, in the oral Torah, the honesty of God is flexible. The oral Torah teaches that God can tell a lie—specifically, that he bears false witness, breaking one of his own Ten Commandments. Rabbi Yishmael says it this way:

> Great is peace, as even the Holy One, blessed be He, departed from the truth for it. As, initially it is written that Sarah said of Abraham: "And my lord is old" (Genesis 18:12), and in the end it is written that God told Abraham that Sarah said: "And I am old" (Genesis 18:13). God adjusted Sarah's words in order to spare Abraham hurt feelings that might lead Abraham and Sarah to quarrel. (Yevamot 65: b)

We can see that this is a complete departure from the heavy emphasis the Tanakh puts on the honesty of God. In the oral Torah, God is okay with lying and breaking the Ten Commandments so as not to hurt someone's feelings and start an argument. At this point in the narrative, Abraham was ninety-nine years old. He had been old for a long time and likely knew he was old. At ninety-nine years, it probably wouldn't have hurt Abraham's feelings to find out that his wife thought he was too old to have a baby. Rabbi Yishmael's quotation is a distortion of the biblical text; he only included part of what Sarah said. Let's see the whole conversation, and you decide if God lied or bore honest witness.

> **Sarah laughed to herself, saying, "After I have become old, am I to have pleasure, my lord being old also?" But YHWH said to Abraham, "Why did Sarah laugh, saying, 'Shall I actually give birth to a child, when I am so old?' Is anything too difficult for YHWH? At the appointed time I will return to you, at this time next year, and Sarah will have a son." Sarah denied it, however, saying, "I did not laugh"; for she was afraid. And He said, "No, but you did laugh."** (Gen. 18:12–15)

Rabbi Yishmael is the one who departed from the truth of Sarah's words, not YHWH. Sarah did not believe God that she would have a child at her advanced age. Yes, she also mentioned Abraham's age, but that was an afterthought to her. We further see that God is not concerned with hurting anyone's feelings here. Sarah did not believe God, and that was a significant problem to him, so he addressed it and pulled no punches. You can almost feel the tension and awkwardness of the situation yourself as you read it. Sarah denied she had laughed; God said, **"No, but you did."** Even in this passage where the oral Torah tries to show that it's okay to lie sometimes, even for God, the text is really conveying that God never lies, and he won't let Sarah get away with it either.

Historical Evidence that the Oral Tradition Is a Later Fabrication

The Art of Oral Tradition

Many cultures have passed down their history through oral tradition. Historians and sociologists have well studied the science of oral tradition. Its reliability is fascinating. Some ignorant skeptics claim oral tradition is like a game of telephone: There's no way to corroborate the history because it's not written. To that, I would ask you to recite Jack and Jill. If you don't know it, ask a friend. In fact, ask two or three friends to corroborate the tale and get to the bottom of what the correct version is. One friend might make a mistake, but you'll discover the correct tale quickly if you ask a few friends. See, you've participated in an oral tradition that is over 175 years old—and you've done so even though you live in a written culture. Oral tradition is far more effective in oral cultures than written ones. Since the majority of people in these cultures can't read and write, they start training how to remember oral traditions at a young age.

There is a particular artful formula that these effective oral traditions across all oral cultures employ that allows them to be effective. The *Encylopedia Britannica* says:

> Notwithstanding their tremendous diversity, oral traditions share certain characteristics across time and space. Most notably, they are rule-governed. They use special languages and performance arenas while employing flexible patterns and structures that aid composition, retention, and reperformance.[4]

For cultures that have oral traditions and written records, the oral tradition is always the poetically condensed version that is easier to remember. And the written version expands upon the oral. So, if the Jewish oral tradition was not a later forgery, you would expect the written version to be much longer than the oral tradition. You'd expect the oral tradition to be poetic, to follow a "highly systematic form of expression, the special oral language of formulaic phrases."[5]

Instead, the supposed Jewish oral tradition far surpasses in size not only the Torah, but also the Prophets and the Writings altogether. And it's not even close. I'm sure you've seen a Tanakh or even a Christian Bible with Old and New Testaments. They're easily contained in the binding of one book. But the volumes of the Talmud alone would take up an entire shelf on a large bookshelf—and remember, the Talmud is hardly a comprehensive collection of the oral tradition. We have to make room for the Zohar, the Mishnah Torah, Maimonides' Guide for the Perplexed, and many, many more.

Next, remember the poetic and highly systematic language historians have discovered in all reliable oral traditions? This linguistic practice is entirely absent from the Jewish oral tradition. In fact, the language of the Jewish oral tradition is much clunkier and inconsistent than in the Tanakh.[6] The oral tradition actually seems to miss the meanings of these repeated phrases.[7] We know that ancient Hebrew had the capacity for such language because the Tanakh uses it. The Tanakh uses this linguistic tool since it was intended to be read aloud, and these repetitions would serve as a memory aid for those who couldn't read. The Tanakh introduces many phrases and themes in Genesis 1 that are woven through the entire Tanakh to call previous passages and meanings to mind, similar to that of a reliable oral tradition. An example would be the "seeing of good and evil and "taking" instead of trusting in God's "giving" that we've already started tracking (Gen. 3, Abraham and Sarah, King David). This style is absent in the so-called oral tradition. The supposed oral tradition does not follow the well-established historical precedent for oral tradition; it doesn't even resemble it.

Since the Jewish oral tradition does not even begin to display any of the features of oral traditions common to the relevant different cultures throughout history, clearly it is not reliable as such. This unreliability is further evidenced by the differences between the Babylonian and Jerusalem Talmuds, which were written only a few hundred years after the Pharisees had begun to invent their content.

Imagine the discrepancies in this vast library of clunky literature had it truly dated back one thousand four hundred years before being written down.

Ethiopian Jewry

Eitan Bar and Golan Broshi have drawn attention to yet another historical fact that shows the oral Torah must have been created during the second temple period and no earlier.[8] Before the Second Temple period, some Jewish people were exiled to Ethiopia.[9] These Jews remained faithful to their heritage and continued to practice Judaism in exile.[10] However, when they finally returned to Israel in the nineteenth and twentieth centuries, they didn't know anything about the oral Torah.[11] Had the oral Torah been given to Moses or even invented before the Second Temple period, they would have been familiar with its traditions and would have been following its commands. The Ethiopian Jews were not familiar with the oral Torah because it was created during the Second Temple Period.

Thanks to the Ethiopian Jews, we have an even clearer picture of the choice presented to us. If we want to embrace our Jewish identity and live life "the Jewish way," we can't fool ourselves into thinking that following Jewish customs like wearing a kippah or lighting a menorah are the Jewish way. The Jewish way is not following the man-made customs in the oral Torah. While there's nothing wrong with the traditions themselves, the true Jewish way started much earlier than the Pharisees. It started with their ancestors and ours. We can choose to follow the rabbis' version of Judaism, the unlawful oral Law, or we can follow the Torah that was given on Mount Sinai. The natural question should be, "Well, then, what does the Torah actually teach?"

Chapter 3: Summary

Part 1: The oral Torah contradicts events that take place in the written Torah.

1. No biblical character ever shows evidence of knowing about an oral Torah
2. Moses didn't know answers that appear in the oral Torah after the time when he would have been given the oral Torah. So he couldn't have had one (Lev. 24; Num. 9:8; 15; 27)
3. YHWH, Abraham, and King David all disobey the kosher laws of the oral Torah (Gen. 18; 2 Sam. 17:29)

Part 2: The character of God is different in the oral Torah and the written Torah

1. The God of the written Torah creates men and women with equal value, but in the oral Torah women are inferior to men
2. The God of the written Torah has great love and affection for all people. He actually chooses the Jewish people in order to bless all people. But in the oral Torah, gentiles are inferior to Jewish people
3. The God of the written Torah categorically forbids the practice of magic in any context. In the oral Torah magic can be practiced by certain people.
4. The God of the written Torah is fully honest and never tolerates lying. In the oral Torah, God will lie to protect someone's feelings and prevent arguments.

Part 3: Historical problems with the validity of the oral Torah

1. There are rules of oral tradition that the oral Torah should follow or at least mimic if it truly was a reliable oral tradition. Instead, it breaks every one of these rules.
2. The Ethiopian Jews who were exiled before the Second Temple period showed no knowledge of the oral Torah upon their return to Israel. Had the oral Torah been around before

their exile, they would have known of it.

Conclusion: Rabbinical Judaism holds that both the oral Torah and the written Torah are true and inspired by God. But from the contradictions between the oral Torah and the Hebrew Bible to the historical problems the oral Torah presents, it's clear that the oral Torah cannot be authentic Scripture.

4

Judaism According to the Tanakh

The Point of the Tanakh According to Its Narrative

It should be clear by now that the oral Torah is the primary holy book of rabbinic Judaism today, but you and I know it couldn't have been given to Moses on Mount Sinai. The oral Torah is the lens that rabbinic Judaism uses to interpret the written Torah and all of the Tanakh. Yet, upon examination, it's evident that the teachings of the oral Torah are incompatible with the Tanakh.

So if those of us who are Jewish want to embrace our Jewish identity, we have a choice. We can choose to follow the rabbis' version of Judaism according to the oral Law. Or we can follow the Tanakh, which includes the Torah given to Moses on Mount Sinai; the Prophets calling people back to that Torah; and the Wisdom Literature that communicates the will of God and teaches us more about him. As we've seen, the oral Torah often misinterprets and even twists the Tanakh, so if we look at the Tanakh without the lens of the oral Torah, we'll see a very different message. Let's dive into the Tanakh and take a look at what it teaches about the Jewish life.

The Tanakh was not always in the bound form of a book that we think of today. It first existed as a collection of scrolls. These scrolls were finalized and set in their order of Torah, Prophets, and Writings sections during the Second Temple period.[1] Much of the time in the Tanakh, the narrative takes center stage, and we follow the story looking for the message that the report intends to convey. Sometimes, though, when the writer doesn't want us to miss something important, the report itself slips into the background, and the author's commentary takes front and center. At the beginnings and endings of each of the three sections, Torah, Prophets, and Writings, the narrators' voices grow especially loud as they tell us what the whole section, and even the whole Tanakh, is about.

Torah
Genesis, Exodus, Leviticus, Numbers, Deuteronomy
Nevi'im—The Prophets
Joshua, Judges, Samuel, Kings
Isaiah, Jeremiah, Ezekiel
The Scroll of the Twelve: Hosea, Joel, Amos, Obadiah, Jonah, Micah, Nahum, Habakkuk, Zephaniah, Haggai, Zechariah, Malachi
Ketuvim—The Writings
Psalms, Job, Proverbs
"The Megillot": Ruth, Song of Songs, Ecclesiastes, Lamentations, Esther
Daniel, Ezra-Nehemiah, Chronicles

Christian readers might find this chart confusing, as Christians have ordered the scrolls differently in the Old Testament and divided some into multiple books, such as Samuel, Kings, and the Scroll of the Twelve.

Humanity Has a Problem Because Humans Sinned

We began the first section by looking at the beginning of the Torah. We'll quickly refresh ourselves on how the narrative was developing and see how it continues. Then we'll look at how the narrators interpreted the stories they were telling. Then we'll look at what the prophets add to the portrait. And finally, we'll analyze how all of these pieces fit together neatly.

The narrative storyline began with God creating the world and making it a good place for humans. God provided good things for humans in abundance, and he is the only one who is supposed to decide what is good and evil. We understand this by tracking the words "see" and "good" through the creation story (Gen. 2:18).

Then God gave the humans a choice that was represented by a tree. They could trust that God truly was good and had their best interests at heart, and they could obey him; or they could decide what was good for themselves and take it by taking from the tree God had told them to refrain from. Instead of trusting God, they listened to a deceiver and took the fruit because he convinced them it would make them like God (Gen. 3:1–6). The great irony here is that they were already made in the image of God (Gen. 1:27).

After the humans made their choice to define good and evil for themselves, God explained more about the consequences of their sin, using the language of curses and blessings. We see that as rulers of the earth, they didn't just affect themselves when they sinned. They actually brought evil into the whole creation, and everything and everyone became affected by it. But while God was explaining the consequences of their sin, he also introduced his plan to fix the evil problem that was now corrupting his creation. God told the deceiver that he would be defeated by the woman's descendant.

> "I will make enemies of you and the woman,
> And of your offspring and her Descendant;
> He shall bruise you on the head,
> And you shall bruise Him on the heel."
>
> (Gen. 3:15)

God Plans to Undo the Problem with Eve's Descendant

As the narrative continues, it zooms in closer and closer on specific descendants of the woman. Remember, the plot began like most stories: Everything was at peace. This peace in the garden lasted until humans sinned; enter plot conflict. Because of their rebellion, humans began to die and were sent away from God's presence. But God immediately revealed a plan to use the woman's offspring to defeat evil.

So, following the plot development, we should naturally be looking for how God is going to use the woman's descendant to fix the problem—that is, death and separation from God.

As the story progresses, we see that we are reading about a specific family that gets narrower and narrower. It becomes clear that the authors wrote about this family to trace the lineage of the descendant God promised Eve at the beginning of the plot conflict. Why are the authors following the lineage of this singular descendant? Because God promised he would be the one to bring resolution to the conflict. God promises him as the solution to evil itself.

So, Abram is one of the first descendants who gets the promised-descendant spotlight. It's clear that Abram is introduced as God's first step in the plan to undo the curses that Adam and Eve brought to creation (Gen. 12:1–3). The line of this future offspring who's going to defeat the deceiver is getting more precise. God tells Abram that the promised offspring will come through his descendants specifically. The Tanakh introduces Abram as the first step in God's plan to undo the curses of sin, namely death and separation from God (Gen. 3:19–24). God explains that Abram will be a blessing to the nations, and his own descendants will themselves become a great nation.

So, we know this blessing or undoing of the curse will come through Abram's descendants. This understanding is highlighted by God changing his name from Abram, which means "Exalted Father to Abraham, "Father of a Multitude of Nations."

But remember, at this point we know we're waiting for one specific descendant of Eve. So we're learning that God has chosen Abraham to use one of his future offspring to undo all evil—for everyone, not just

Abraham's descendants. You can see this even as early as God's first call to Abram.

> "Go from your country,
> And from your relatives
> And from your father's house,
> To the land which I will show you;
> And I will make you into a great nation,
> And I will bless you,
> And make your name great;
> And you shall be a blessing;
> And I will bless those who bless you,
> And the one who curses you I will curse.
> And in you all the families of the earth will be blessed."
>
> (Gen. 12:1–3)

The narrative continues. The people of Israel grow into a nation enslaved in Egypt. But God remembers his promise to Abraham and brings Israel out of Egypt and makes a covenant with them. It's through this covenant that the people of Israel are reminded of their purpose. When God made his promise to Abraham, he explained that he was going to make Abraham a great nation in order to use Abraham to bless all the nations of the earth (Gen. 12:3). God reminds the whole people of Israel about this purpose when he tells them:

> "'If you will indeed obey My voice and keep My covenant, then you shall be My own possession among all the peoples, for all the earth is Mine; and you shall be to Me a kingdom of priests and a holy nation.' These are the words that you shall speak to the sons of Israel." (Ex. 19:5–6)

Notice that Israel is supposed to be a kingdom of priests. The role of priests includes teaching and maintaining the Torah, but their job mainly involves intervening on behalf of the people. The work of the priests is largely to keep away the punishment that Israel earns by sinning. Let's take a look at the role of priests according to the narrator, and at how Israel's role as a nation of priests fit into the larger story.

> "You shall perform the duties of the sanctuary and the duties of the altar, so that there will no longer be wrath on the sons of Israel. Behold, I Myself have taken your fellow Levites from among the sons of Israel; they are a gift to you, dedicated to YHWH, to perform the service for the tent of meeting." (Num. 18:5-6; see also Ex. 30:10)

Also, note that the priests work in the "tent of meeting." Meeting who? The narrative makes it clear that the tent of meeting (and later the temple) is where God's personal presence dwells. So, the priest is able to go in and meet with the presence of God, but only after he makes a sacrifice to atone for his own sins. And another to atone for the sins of the people (Lev.16:11-17).

In Exodus 19:6, God tells all of Israel that he plans on using them as a kingdom of priests if they keep all of his commands. So, now we know what priests do and that Israel is supposed to be a kingdom of priests. This teaches that, functioning as priests, Israel is going to help undo the curses of sin, namely death and separation from God. They'll keep the curse away by doing what God instructed them to do. That is to say, they'll be priests for the world if they keep the covenant. But we know that they don't keep the covenant.

> "Behold, days are coming," declares YHWH, "when I will make a new covenant with the house of Israel and the house of Judah, not like the covenant which I made with their fathers on the day I took them by the hand to bring them out of the land of Egypt, My covenant which they broke, although I was a husband to them." (Jer. 31:31-32; cf. Deut.31:16, Jdg. 2:20, Dan. 9:5-6,11, Neh. 1:6-7)

Okay, so Israel doesn't keep the covenant. So they don't get to be a kingdom of priests the way God intended for them. Still, God doesn't give up on them, because even though that covenant was conditional on their obedience, the promise he made to Eve and then Abraham was unconditional. So he's still going to use them to undo the sin problem.

We keep following the narrative. More promises are woven through the story, and we keep getting more details about the genealogy of the woman's offspring. We know he's going to come through the line of Shem. (Gen. 9:27). Then we find out he will come through the line of Judah (Gen. 49:9–10; Num. 23:9). Then the line becomes much narrower: God promises that it will be King David's descendant who's going to take care of the sin problem and rule forever

> "Behold, the days are coming," declares YHWH,
> "When I will raise up for David a righteous Branch;
> And He will reign as king and act wisely
> And do justice and righteousness in the land.
> In His days Judah will be saved,
> And Israel will live securely;
> And this is His name by which He will be called,
> 'YHWH Our Righteousness.'"
>
> (Jeremiah 23:5-6; cf. 2 Sam. 7:12–16)

Did the Jewish prophet Jeremiah, who lived around 687–587 BCE, just say that the kingly descendant of David would be called by the same name as God himself?[2] The same name that is considered so special and holy to God that many Jewish people today won't even say it out loud, but instead replace it with "Hashem" or "Adonai" because it's so sacred? Yes, he did.

So far, we've been calling this person we're waiting for "Eve's future descendant" or "the offspring." But as we follow the narrative, we keep getting more and more information about what he's going to be like and what he'll do. For example, we already know that in addition to being a descendant of Eve, Abraham, Isaac, Jacob, Judah, and David, he will be a righteous king.

It's clear that the Tanakh is building expectation for this person. It would be helpful if there was a specific title for him, so we don't have to call him "the offspring" or "the descendant" every time. But the Tanakh doesn't use one specific title for this person every time. It calls him by many different names: the Son of Man, the root of Jesse, Messiah, and more (Dan. 7:13; 9:25; Is. 11:10). Often the Tanakh doesn't use any title at all; it just talks about what he's going to do (Gen. 3:15; Deut. 18:15–19). The ancient Jewish world must have felt the same way about using one primary title for him, because they started to mainly refer to him as "Messiah."[3]

Messiah makes sense; it means "anointed one." Anointing someone was the practice of pouring oil on their head to symbolize that they were chosen by God to be either a king, a high priest, or a prophet. (Lev. 18:12; 1 Sam. 10:1; 16:10; 1 Kings 19:6). So it would make sense to call this future descendant the Messiah, because he would be all three: king, prophet, and priest (Deut. 18:15–19; 2 Sam. 7:12–16; Ps. 110:4). From here on out, we'll mostly refer to Eve's snake-crushing descendant as the Messiah.

We already know a lot about what the Messiah will do. Because humanity sinned, they have a problem, namely, evil in the world, death, and separation from God, who created humans to be with him (Is. 59:2). The Messiah is going to undo all that by taking care of their sin, just like a priest does (Is. 53:5; Ps. 110:4). He will be king over Israel and establish peace on earth (Is. 9:6). At this point, it should start occurring to us that the peace he's going to establish has more to do with peace between God and humans than between humans and each other. However, the promise is that he will bring both kinds of peace (Is. 9:6–7).

The Point of the Tanakh According to Its Narrators

Occasionally, as mentioned earlier, the authors of the Tanakh take center stage, and the narrative slips into the background momentarily. The authors do this to make sure we are getting the point. So, just to be sure we're not missing the point here, let's step back from the narrative for a moment, and check what the authors of the Hebrew Bible think the story is actually about. At the beginning and the end of each collection, the writers insert themselves to remind us what their purpose is so we don't get lost in the details. We'll look at the key moments when the narrators step forward with commentary and direct our attention.

Tanakh authors stepping forward as narrators and linking everything together as one story

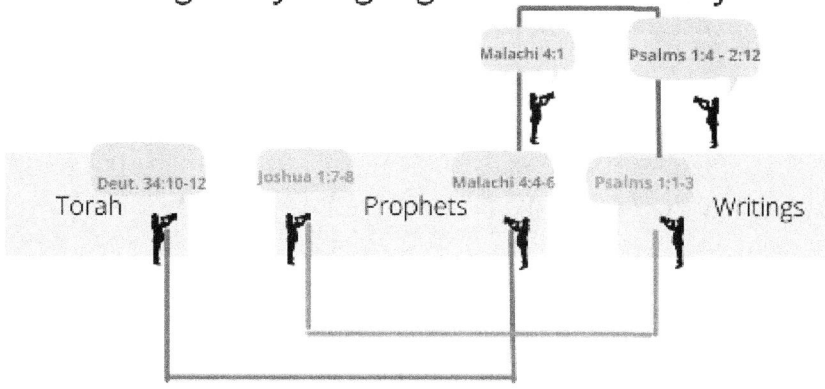

This chart shows the key points when the authors take center stage to make sure we get the point. Notice this occurs at the beginning and end of each section.

Internal Commentary of the Tanakh

The narrators of the Tanakh step forward in Deuteronomy 34:10–12, Joshua 1:7–8, Malachi 4:4–6, and Psalms 1–2 to link its three collections together and show that what connects them is their shared message.

The Torah and the Prophets are linked together at their respective ends by showing that after everything they just wrote about, you should still be waiting for the future prophet who will be king (Deut. 34:10-12; Mal. 4:4-6). The beginning of the Prophets and the beginning of the Writings are linked together by the identical language used to describe what the ideal leader of Israel will be like (Josh. 1:7–8; Psalm 1:1–3). The end of the Prophets and the beginning of the Writings are linked together as well, neatly tying all of this together. This last link shows that God's plan to get rid of evil is to make his Son king and separate the good from the wicked (Pss. 1:4–2:12).

Taking all of this together as the authors intended, we can see that this whole Tanakh is about God's plan to deal with evil, and he will do it by sending his Son as a prophet to be a good king who will separate the good from the wicked. Let's dive in and look at these links.

End of the Torah and End of the Prophets

The first subcollection in the larger collection called the TaNaK is the Torah. The narrative of the Torah ends with the death of Moses. Directly after, in the very last sentences of the Torah, the narrator takes center stage and tells readers,

> Since that time no prophet has risen in Israel like Moses, whom YHWH knew face to face, for all the signs and wonders which YHWH sent him to perform in the land of Egypt against Pharaoh, all his servants, and all his land—and for all the mighty power and all the great terror which Moses performed in the sight of all Israel. (Deut 34: 10–12)

The end of the Torah—that's a pretty disappointing ending. All of those great things Moses did . . . awesome. And by the way, nobody has ever done that again. The end.

Why did the authors feel the right way to end this amazing narrative about the creation of the world, the separation of God and humans, and God's plan to fix that problem with a future messianic person was to say, "Oh yeah, and there hasn't been anybody like Moses ever since"?

To understand that, we have to turn back a few pages to the last time we see the phrase "a prophet like Moses." The phrase is used twice in Deuteronomy 18:

> "YHWH your God will raise up for you a prophet like me [Moses speaking to Israel] from among you, from your countrymen; to him you shall listen." (v. 15)

"I [YHWH speaking to Moses] will raise up for them a prophet from among their countrymen like you, and I will put My words in his mouth, and he shall speak to them everything that I command him. And it shall come about that whoever does not listen to My words which he speaks in My name, I Myself will require [*edros*] it of him." (vv. 18–19)

So, near the end of the Torah, God tells Moses that in the future he will raise up a prophet like Moses, and that prophet will speak the words God tells him to speak. God makes it clear that it will be important to listen to this prophet. The Hebrew word for "require it" is *edros*, which means "to be held responsible." It's an accusatory word (see Ezek. 33:6; Gen. 9:5). God promises to raise up another prophet like Moses, but not all the people of Israel will listen to this prophet. The people who don't will be held accountable.

Now flip back to the very end of the Torah and read what the narrators want us to chew on as we close the book and reflect on what we've read. They want us to finish the Torah thinking about this future prophet, the promised one who would be like Moses. The narrators see the whole story of the Torah—or at least what we should be thinking about when we finish it—as being about the prophet who will be like Moses and hasn't yet come.

End of the Prophets and Beginning of the Writings

Next, let's flip to the end of the Prophets [Nevi'im] section of the taNak to see what the narrators have to say there. And get ready for an overload of the word *prophet*. We'll be talking about the Prophets section of the Tanakh; about the prophet who will be like Moses; and about yet another prophet who will announce the Moses-like prophet.

"Remember the Law [Torah] of Moses My servant, the statutes and ordinances which I commanded him in Horeb for all Israel.

> "Behold, I am going to send you Elijah the prophet before the coming of the great and terrible day of YHWH. He will turn the hearts of the fathers back to their children and the hearts of the children to their fathers, so that I will not come and strike the land with complete destruction."
> (Mal. 4:4–6)

Similar to the Torah, the Prophets end with the narrators telling us to wait for a future prophet. But this time, the prophet we're told to wait for is called Elijah, not Moses. They note that he will call the people back to the Torah and restore the hearts of Israel before the Day of YHWH. As you read through the prophets, "the Day of YHWH" is a term used repeatedly, and we learn a lot about what it means.

The Day of YHWH is basically a day of judgment when the Messiah (root of Jesse) will begin his rule. When that day comes, God will judge the wicked for their wickedness and heal everyone who fears or reveres the name of God. The Day of YHWH is a time when the wicked are separated from the good and the Messiah begins his rule (Mal. 4:1–3; Isa. 11:10). As you read the Prophets, it becomes clear that the people who are being healed are healed from the consequences of evil in the world. So, this is talking about a day when evil is removed from creation.

How does God say he will determine who's good and who's wicked on that day? The person who reveres God and gives allegiance to his chosen king is counted "righteous" or good, and the rest are wicked (Mal. 4:1–2).

So, the Prophets section of the Tanakh ends in a similar fashion to the Torah section by telling us to wait for another prophet to come. The narrators tell us that this prophet will be announcing the Day of YHWH—the day of judgment, when the Messiah will begin reigning over his kingdom (Isa. 11:10). What the narrators want us to think about as we finish the Prophets section is the prophet who is going to announce the day of YHWH.

We finish the Torah section with the narrators framing the whole story as being about the coming prophet who will be like Moses. We learn that he's the Messiah, because people will be judged based on their response to him, which is how Malachi describes the Messiah's reign. Then we finish the Prophets section with the narrators framing it in the same storyline, waiting for the Day of YHWH, the day when the Messiah will start reigning.

At the end of the Prophets, the narrators tell us to keep waiting for the prophet like Moses to come. But now they add that when the Messiah comes, another prophet with the spirit of Elijah will announce him. What the narrators want us to be thinking about when we finish the Prophets section of the Tanakh is again the future prophet (the Messiah) who the Torah is all about, who hasn't come yet. They give us more information about his arrival: He'll be announced by another prophet with the spirit of Elijah (Mal. 4:1–2; 2 Kings 2:9–15).

If you're not convinced that these sections are linked, hang in there and wait for the beginning of the Writings section. That section neatly ties all three sections together. But, before we get there, let's examine the beginning of the Prophets section. The authors intentionally put a link there for us to find that launches us into the Writings section.

Beginning of the Prophets and Beginning of the Writings

At the endings of the Torah and the Prophets, the narrators linked the stories together by reminding us to keep waiting for the Moses-like prophet. Now we'll look at the beginning of the Prophets and the beginning of the Writings section, where the narrators shout even more clues about what these collections are about. Spoiler alert: The narrators continue to connect these collections by linking them through the prophet who will be like Moses.

On the first page of the Prophets, God speaks to Joshua, who will be the next leader. God tells Joshua that he will be kind of like Moses. But we know he's not *the* one like Moses, because when the Torah ends, it says, *"Since that time* no prophet has arisen like Moses" (Deut. 34:10, emphasis mine), and Joshua was around during the time of Moses. He starts leading the Jewish people immediately after

Moses dies. The authors wouldn't have said "since that time" if they were talking about Joshua. Nevertheless, even though Joshua isn't *the* prophet like Moses, he is kind of like Moses. Moreover, like Elijah, he can reveal more about what the future prophet will be like—because if the prophet is like Moses, and if Joshua is also kind of like Moses, then *the* Moses-like prophet will also resemble Joshua.

On the first page of the Prophets, God tells Joshua how to be a good leader. The narrators use this command given in the very beginning of the Prophets section as a literary link, to the very opening lines of the Writings section.

Now we know what God expects a good leader of the Jewish people to be like. They'll be strong and courageous, obey all of the Torah, and meditate on the Torah day and night. Now it's time to see what the authors of the last section of the Tanakh think this is all about.

The Writings section opens with the following lines. Compare them to the beginning of the Prophets, where we learn what God expects a good leader of Israel to be like.

> Blessed is the person who *does not walk in the counsel of the wicked,*
> Nor stand in the path of sinners,
> Nor sit in the seat of scoffers!
> But *his delight is in the Law of YHWH,*
> And *on His Law he meditates day and night.*
> He will be like a tree planted by streams of water,
> Which yields its fruit in its season,
> And its leaf does not wither;
> And in whatever he does, he *prospers.*
>
> (Ps. 1:1–3, connections to Josh. Italicized)

> "Be strong and very courageous. Be careful to obey all the Law which My servant Moses commanded you; *do not turn from it to the right or to the left,* that you may achieve success wherever you go. This *Book of the Law shall not*

depart from your mouth, but you shall *meditate on it day and night*, so that you may be careful to do according to all that is written in it; for then you will make your way *prosperous*, and then you will achieve *success*." (Josh. 1: 7–8, connections to Ps. Italicized)

The narrators are clearly linking these two passages together. They essentially copy-and-pasted from the Joshua scroll and made it sound more poetic for the psalm. This psalm was written hundreds of years after Joshua died, so we can learn that this command for a good leader is not just for Joshua. The narrators have already linked the end of the Torah to the end of the Prophets, so we know this whole story is about the same thing. The fact that they also link the beginning of the Prophets to the beginning of the Writings connects the Writings section to the whole overarching story. The narrators don't connect these stories using some random section; they link them together with the main theme of Israel's ideal leader.

Let's read more from the first page of the Writings to see if the narrators tell us anything else about this leader.

> The wicked are not so,
> But they are like chaff which the wind blows away.
> Therefore the wicked will not stand in the judgment,
> Nor sinners in the assembly of the righteous.
> For YHWH knows the way of the righteous,
> But the way of the wicked will perish.
>
> (Ps. 1:4–6)

This is the end of the same psalm that the narrators used to link the Writings section to the beginning of the Prophets. Now it's being used to link to the *end* of the Prophets. This is extra confirmation that the stories are all tied together. And the key theme that unites them? It's this ideal, future leader-prophet-king of Israel we've been waiting for since God's promise to Eve.

The part of Psalm 1 about the chaff being blown away is the same language the narrators used at the end of the Prophets section: "Every evildoer will be chaff; and the day that is coming will set them ablaze" (Mal. 4:1). The end of the Prophets draws a contrast between the good and the wicked and what will happen to them, and we see the same contrast in Psalm 1. The language is so similar that it's clear the narrators expect us to mentally link them together as messages that interact to give a fuller picture. So, we can see the narrators are telling us that this collection of Writings, which is being tied to the Torah and Prophets, is also about what will happen to the good people and the bad people. Malachi tells us that what makes someone good is, that person fears YHWH's name. And the whole collection has to do with the coming day of YHWH, which has now been tied together with the prophet who will be like Moses. Let's continue reading the first page of the Writings, because the authors tell us more about what the entire Tanakh is about.

> Why are the nations restless
> And the peoples plotting in vain?
> The kings of the earth take their stand
> And the rulers conspire together
> Against YHWH and against His Anointed [Messiah], saying,
> "Let's tear their shackles apart
> And throw their ropes away from us!"
>
> (Ps. 2: 1–2)

The narrators are reminding us of the sin problem, which is essentially a rebellion against God that gets worse and worse. People have decided they, not God, should be the ones to define good and evil. But

> He who sits in the heavens laughs,
> The Lord scoffs at them.
> Then He will speak to them in His anger
> And terrify them in His fury, saying,
> "But as for Me, I have installed My King

Upon Zion, My holy mountain."

(Ps. 2:4-6)

God is not at all worried about this human rebellion because he has a plan. Here we should remember God's promise to David about putting an anointed king on the throne of Israel to reign forever. That is God's response to the human sin problem: Put a king on the throne. How does God refer to this king?

"I will announce the decree of YHWH:
He said to Me, 'You are My Son,
Today I have fathered You.
Ask it of Me, and I will certainly give the nations as Your inheritance,
And the ends of the earth as Your possession.'"

(Ps. 2:7–9)

God refers to this king as his own Son, who he will give not just Israel but the entire earth. He is more than a king—he is *the* King, God's Son. And all people are going to be ruled by God's Son-King.

"'You shall break them with a rod of iron,
You shall shatter them like earthenware.'"
Now then, you kings, use insight;
Let yourselves be instructed, you judges of the earth.
Serve YHWH with reverence
And rejoice with trembling.
Kiss [*nashak*] the Son, that He not be angry and you perish on the way, For His wrath may be kindled quickly.
How blessed are all who take refuge in Him!

(Ps. 2:9–12)

We've seen that the consequences of sin are death and separation from God. Here the narrators link together the three collections of the Tanakh to reveal the Prophet-Leader who will heal creation. Specifically, he's going to heal humans who are suffering as a result of evil, and he will remove the wicked from creation. The reader is told how to receive this healing and avoid being dashed to pieces and destroyed: "Kiss the Son."

We know who the Son is from earlier in the same passage: God says he will install an anointed (literally "Messiah" in Heb.) King who is going to be His Son. Why do we have to kiss him? That's weird. The Hebrew word *nashak*, translated here as "kiss," is also often translated as "pay homage." Even when it's translated as "kiss," it's often a symbolic act of paying homage to a king. (See Gen. 41:40; 1 Sam. 10:1; 1 Kings 19:18). It literally means "kiss," but it's referring to giving allegiance. By kissing the Son-King, you are expressing your allegiance to him.

The narrators of the Tanakh believed all three sections were connected to each other. And they linked each section together at the beginning and end of each section, exactly where you'd expect a narrator to take center stage and explain the text to you. (You see the same thing when you watch a narrated movie in our culture: The narrator steps forward in the beginning to set the scene, and is the one who explains the moral at the end.) The narrators explain to us that all three collections are linked together by the intended message, which revolves around the Prophet who will be like Moses, and who will be announced by someone who, like Elijah, is given the Spirit of God.

It's about God's plan to rid his creation of the evil humans brought into it. He'll do so by separating the good from the wicked. He qualifies the righteous as those who fear his name. Specifically, the righteous are those who give their allegiance to his Son, the King he has chosen.

What Prophecies Add to the Message of the Tanakh

By following the story laid out in the narrative, we've tracked the developing conflict and God's plan to resolve it. We've seen that God created humans to be rulers over the earth under his authority, and when they sinned, they polluted the world, doomed themselves to death, and were separated from God. God revealed his plan to fix the sin problem by using the descendant of Eve, specifically someone who would come through the line of David. He would be a King, and he would also fulfill the function of Priest that Israel was supposed to perform (Isaiah 53:5, Ps. 110:4). Remember, that priests teach the Torah and perform sacrifices that somehow atone for the people's sin so that they no longer are separated from God but can meet with him personally.

Then we tracked what the narrators told us about the intended meaning of the whole Tanakh. They agreed with our interpretation. They connected the whole point of the Tanakh by linking all of it through the promised future Prophet, who would also be the King who'd fix the problem of sin and evil. The narrators further told us that the way to be counted righteous will be to give our allegiance to this King, who will be the Son of God.

By now we should have noticed that one and the same person fulfills all these descriptions and functions, which intertwine on many levels. This Messiah figure is going to be the Son of God; he is going to have the role of Priest; he's going to have the Spirit of God; he's going to be King; and he is going to fix the sin problem. The story arc and the narrators of the Tanakh make it clear that the Tanakh is about this one figure who will do all the things we've covered.

While that outline of the Messiah might seem sufficient, the Tanakh is even more specific than what we have seen so far.

—

Let's look at one of the times the prophet Isaiah tells us about the Messiah and what he would be like. We can be sure Isaiah is talking about the Messiah because he's talking about the person who will be given all authority and government, exactly like the person from Psalm 2 who will be God's King.

> A Child will be born to us, a Son will be given to us;
> And the government will rest on His shoulders;
> And His name will be called Wonderful Counselor, Mighty God,

> Eternal Father, Prince of Peace.
> There will be no end to the increase of His government or of peace
> On the throne of David and over his kingdom,
> To establish it and to uphold it with justice and righteousness
> From then on and forevermore.
> The zeal of YHWH of armies will accomplish this.
>
> (Isa. 9:6–7)

From this we learn that the Messiah is going to be born as a child, and he's going to be the King who will rule forever on the throne of David. We also find out more about what he will be called. It's particularly interesting that Isaiah says the Messiah will be called Mighty God and Eternal Father. These are titles that have always been exclusively reserved for YHWH, reserved for God. Is Isaiah telling us that the Messiah not only is going to be born on earth and reign over it forever, but also that he will actually be God himself? He is, and we'll see this confirmed in other prophets.

To summarize, the Messiah—King, Prophet, Priest, and Son of God—will reign forever and usher in peace. But then we also learn he will be punished for the sins of everyone.

This next prophecy tells us a lot about who the Messiah is and what he will do. I encourage you to read through it a few times and pick up as much as you can about what it tells us the Messiah will be like.

> Who has believed our report?
> And to whom has the arm of YHWH been revealed?
> For He grew up before Him like a tender shoot,
> And like a root out of dry ground;
> He has no stately form or majesty
> That we would look at Him,
> Nor an appearance that we would take pleasure in Him.
> He was despised and abandoned by men,

A man of great pain and familiar with sickness;
And like one from whom people hide their faces,
He was despised, and we had no regard for Him.

However, it was our sicknesses that He Himself bore,
And our pains that He carried;
Yet we ourselves assumed that He had been afflicted,
Struck down by God, and humiliated.
But He was pierced for our offenses,
He was crushed for our wrongdoings;
The punishment for our well-being was laid upon Him,
And by His wounds we are healed.
All of us, like sheep, have gone astray,
Each of us has turned to his own way;
But YHWH has caused the wrongdoing of us all
To fall on Him.

He was oppressed and afflicted,
Yet He did not open His mouth;
Like a lamb that is led to slaughter,
And like a sheep that is silent before its shearers,
So He did not open His mouth.
By oppression and judgment He was taken away;
And as for His generation, who considered
That He was cut off from the land of the living
For the wrongdoing of my people, to whom the blow was due?
And His grave was assigned with wicked men,
Yet He was with a rich man in His death,
Because He had done no violence,
Nor was there any deceit in His mouth.

But YHWH desired
To crush Him, causing Him grief;
If He renders Himself as a guilt offering,
He will see His offspring,

> He will prolong His days,
> And the good pleasure of YHWH will prosper in His hand.
> As a result of the anguish of His soul,
> He will see it and be satisfied;
> By His knowledge the Righteous One,
> My Servant, will justify the many,
> For He will bear their wrongdoings.
> Therefore, I will allot Him a portion with the great,
> And He will divide the plunder with the strong,
> Because He poured out His life unto death,
> And was counted with wrongdoers;
> Yet He Himself bore the sin of many,
> And interceded for the wrongdoer
>
> (Isaiah 53)

This prophecy tells us that the Messiah is going to be good, remembering that God's standard for good is never sinning, always letting God define good and evil: "Because He had done no violence, nor was there any deceit in His mouth."

This Messiah, the only righteous person, will justify the many by bearing their wrongdoing himself: "All of us, like sheep, have gone astray, each of us has turned to his own way." "The Righteous One, My Servant, will justify the many, for He will bear their wrongdoings."

How is he going to justify the wrongdoings of the many? He is going to die and be counted as a sinner; he will be a sacrifice so that the sinners will be counted righteous: "He poured out His life unto death, and was counted with wrongdoers; Yet He Himself bore the sin of many, and interceded for the wrongdoers."

This prophecy further tells us that the Messiah will be rejected by the people of his generation. In other words, they won't recognize him as Messiah.

> He has no stately form or majesty
> That we would look at Him,
> Nor an appearance that we would take pleasure in Him.

> He was despised and abandoned by men,
> A man of great pain and familiar with sickness;
> And like one from whom people hide their faces,
> He was despised, and we had no regard for Him.
>
> (vv. 2–3)
>
> And as for His generation, who considered
> That He was cut off from the land of the living.
>
> (v. 8)

We already know the Messiah will reign forever over God's kingdom. Now we discover he is going to be punished in place of the wicked even though he is without sin. It says he's actually going to die to pay the punishment for their sins: "Because He poured out His life unto death." But we also know God must do something to restore his life, because he is going to rule forever—and you can't rule forever if you're dead. Verse 12 hints that God will resurrect him: "I will allot Him a portion with the great, and He will divide the plunder with the strong." Likewise, verse 10—"If He renders Himself as a guilt offering, He will see His offspring, He will prolong His days"—tells us the Messiah will be sacrificed for our sins, but God will extend his days.

Psalm 16 shows us even more about how this will work. Verses 8–11 refer to the Messiah, for, as we've just read in Isaiah 53, all people are sinners except the Righteous One, the Messiah. ("All of us, like sheep, have gone astray, each of us has turned to his own way.") But in Psalm 16, the author uses the same language about a unique holy person. The author calls this person God's "Holy One"; it's a title of sorts. We see that the Messiah will not stay in Sheol (one of the Hebrew Bible's terms for where a person goes when they die; it's portrayed as a place you don't want to go):

> I have set YHWH continually before me;
> Because He is at my right hand, I will not be shaken.
> Therefore my heart is glad and my glory rejoices;

> My flesh also will dwell securely.
> For You will not abandon my soul to Sheol;
> You will not allow Your Holy One to undergo decay.
> You will make known to me the way of life;
> In Your presence is fullness of joy;
> In Your right hand there are pleasures forever.
>
> (Psalm 16:8–11)

This Psalm tells us that the Messiah, the Holy One of God, who we know is without sin yet who will die to pay the punishment all humans deserve, will not stay dead. God is going to bring him back to life.

The prophet Isaiah has told us the Messiah's generation won't recognize him when he comes: "He was despised, and we had no regard for Him." He will be punished for our sins: "He was pierced for our offenses." And he's given names that have been applied only to God, including Mighty God and Eternal Father. Another Jewish prophet of the Tanakh, Zechariah, tells us more about how these things all connect to the larger story:

> "I [God] will pour out on the house of David and on the inhabitants of Jerusalem the Spirit of grace and of pleading, so that they will look at *Me whom they pierced*; and they will mourn for Him, like one mourning for an only son, and they will weep bitterly over Him like the bitter weeping over a firstborn. On that day the mourning in Jerusalem will be great, like the mourning of Hadadrimmon in the plain of Megiddo. The land will mourn, every family by itself." (Zech. 12:10–12, emphasis mine)

Who does God say was pierced? God says it was *himself*, God, who was pierced. In Isaiah, we learned that the Messiah was the one who would be pierced as a sacrifice for our sins. We also learned that he is the only righteous person. Now, knowing that the Messiah is God himself, it makes sense why he would be the only righteous one.

It also begins to make more sense of why, in Psalm 2, God refers to the Messiah as his own Son.

And we can understand why, when he returns, the Jewish people will be bitterly upset, even though God is going to give them grace. They'll realize they did not recognize the Messiah when he came: "He was despised, and [they] had no regard for Him." "They will look at Me whom they pierced" and weep bitterly and sincerely—because they will realize their anointed Messiah loved them so much that he came to pay the punishment for their sins so they could live. They will weep because, after God did all this for them, they rejected him and even despised him.

Does that mean there's no hope for the Jewish people? Is God going to be done with them because he did all that and yet they rejected him? No! He tells them he will still treat them with grace and even plead with them to express their allegiance to him. "And I will pour out on the house of David and on the inhabitants of Jerusalem the Spirit of grace and of pleading,"

Intersection of the Narrative, Narration, and Prophecies
(This is What the Tanakh is About)

By now, we should see how the Tanakh's narrative, its prophecies about the Messiah, and what the narrators expect us to pick up all overlap. They all teach that everyone has sinned, and everyone must deal with the consequences of their sin.

All People Have Earned Death

1. Everyone is Guilty
    - "There is not a righteous person on earth who always does good and does not ever sin." (Eccl. 7:20)
    - "YHWH has looked down from heaven upon the sons of mankind

        To see if there are any who understand,

Who seek God.
They have all turned aside, together they are corrupt;
There is no one who does good, not even one."
(Ps. 14: 2–3)

2. Consequence for Evil is Separation from God and Death
- "Behold, all souls are Mine; the soul of the father as well as the soul of the son is Mine. The soul who sins will die." (Ezek. 18:4)1
- "Your wrongdoings have caused a separation between you and your God" (Isa. 59:2)

According to the Tanakh, all humans have this problem. As sinners, we all are separated from God and will experience the consequence of sin, which is death.

But God also revealed at the beginning of the Torah, and throughout the whole Tanakh, that he had a plan to deal with this sin problem. The Tanakh reveals more and more about this plan, and its culmination is shown to us in Isaiah 53, where we learn that the Messiah would pay the punishment for our sins, even though he himself would be righteous. We know that all humans are sinful, but the Messiah can be righteous because the Prophets teach us that the Messiah will be God himself.

The Messiah Will Be Righteous Because He Will Be God

- "The Righteous One, My Servant, will justify the many,
  For He will bear their wrongdoings."
  (Isa. 53:11)

- "They will look at Me whom they pierced." (Zech. 12:10)
    - "He was pierced for our offenses,
       He was crushed for our wrongdoings;

---

[1] Skolnik, *Encyclopaedia Judaica*, vol. 6. 636. Ezekiel wrote from 593-573 BCE

> The punishment for our well-being was laid upon Him,
> And by His wounds we are healed."
>
> (Isa. 53:5)

God's plan to deal with the sin problem is for himself to be the Messiah, referred to as the Son of God, and die in our place. The Messiah will take the punishment for sin: death. But according to the Tanakh, after the Messiah dies, what happens next?

The Messiah Will Be Resurrected

- "If He renders Himself as a guilt offering,
  He will see His offspring,
  He will prolong His days."

  (Isaiah 53:10)

- "For You will not abandon my soul to Sheol;
  You will not allow Your Holy One to undergo decay."

  (Ps. 16:10)

Some Will Reject the Resurrected Messiah, but Those Who Follow Him Will Have Eternal Life

1. Some will reject him.
   - "As for His generation, who considered
     That He was cut off from the land of the living."

     (Isa. 53:8)

   - "He was despised, and we had no regard for Him." (Isa. 53:3)

2. Those who reject him will die.
   - "Kiss the Son, that He not be angry and you perish on the way" (Ps. 2:12)
   - "Behold, the day is coming, burning like a furnace; and all the arrogant and every evildoer will be chaff; and the day that is

coming will set them ablaze," says YHWH of armies, "so that it will leave them neither root nor branches." (Mal. 4:1)

3. Those who follow him will have eternal life.
- "The punishment for our well-being was laid upon Him, And by His wounds we are healed."

(Isa. 53:5)

- "Everyone who is found written in the book, will be rescued. And many of those who sleep in the dust of the ground will awake, these to everlasting life, but the others to disgrace and everlasting contempt." (Dan. 12:1–2)

To summarize what we've seen: The Tanakh is about God's good world, in which he designed humans to dwell with him for eternity. But they rebelled against God and brought evil into the world. The Tanakh teaches that everyone has sinned and brought evil into the world in one way or another. It further teaches that God's plan for dealing with the sin problem is to come to the earth as a baby ("A child will be born to us, a son will be given to us; and the government will rest on His shoulders"), and, as the Messiah, to pay the punishment for our sins by dying ("He poured out His life unto death"). After the Messiah dies, God, his Father, will honor his sacrifice by resurrecting him ("If He renders Himself as a guilt offering, He will see His offspring, He will prolong His days"). Everyone who trusts in what God did by coming as the Messiah and dying to pay the punishment we earned for our sins will have eternal life. And those that don't will not experience eternal life; instead, those who reject him will experience the death every one of us earned, even though Messiah paid for it.

It starts to become clear that the Bible is a love letter written by a God who will give everything to rescue his people without forcing anyone to follow him.

Do you remember how the Rabbinic Jewish traditions hold that the teachings of the Tanakh are accurate and true? Well, this is the teaching of the Tanakh. Unfortunately, the Rabbinic traditions are mistakenly looking at the Tanakh through the lens of the man-made oral Torah, and it guides them away from the message of the Tanakh.

If the Messiah paid the punishment for sin, why do the people who continue to reject God and reject the Son of God still have to die? In the garden of Eden, God wanted humans to have the ability to freely choose either to trust his definition of good and evil or to decide good and evil for themselves. A tree represented this choice. God won't force anyone into a relationship with him. If they prefer to remain separated from him, even after he died for them, he will let them. Just like a tree represented the first choice, the choice that we have now is again represented by a tree.

Chapter 4: Summary

Part 1: The point of the Tanakh according to its narrative.

1. Humanity has a problem because humans sinned and keep on sinning (Gen. 3:6; 4:6–8; Jer. 31:32)
   a. Evil is in the world (Gen. 6:5).
   b. People die (Gen. 3:19; Ezek. 18:4).
   c. Humans are separated from the God they were created to be with (Gen. 3:23-24; Isa. 59:2).

2. God's plan to undo this is through the offspring of Eve, specifically through David (Gen. 3:15; Isa. 9:7; 11:1; Jer. 23:5-6).
   a. This offspring is going to undo the damage. Like a priest, he's going to take care of humans' sin (Isa. 53:12; Ps. 110:4; Lev. 4:16-20).
   a. He's going to be a King over Israel and establish peace on earth. That peace consists primarily of restoring the relationship between God and humans (Gen. 3:15; Isa. 9:6; 53; Ps. 2:6-7, 12)

Part 2: The point of the Tanakh according to its narrators.

1. All three collections of the Tanakh (Torah, Prophets, and the Writings) are linked together by their shared intended message.

2. Their message revolves around a Prophet who is going to be like Moses.

3. The narrators explain that the Tanakh is about God's plan to rid his creation of the evil humans brought into creation. He will accomplish this by separating the good from the wicked.

4. God will qualify who is righteous by counting those who fear his name as righteous

5. Specifically, those that are counted righteous are those who give their allegiance to God's Son, the King he's chosen.

Part 3: What Prophecies add to the message of the Tanakh.

1. The Messiah will be born as a child and will reign forever. He is referred to by names typically only used for God (Isa. 9:6).

2. The Messiah will offer himself up as a sacrifice.
   a. He will be righteous (Isa. 53:11. Zech. 12:10).
   b. He will be rejected and despised by his own generation (Isa. 53:3, 8).
   c. He will nevertheless let himself die to pay for the punishment sinners have earned for themselves (Isa. 53:3–4).
   d. Many sinners who have earned death will instead experience healing and life as a result of his sacrifice (Dan. 12:1–2).

3. After sacrificing himself, the Messiah will be raised from the dead by God (Isa. 53:12; Ps. 16:10).

4. Everyone who trusts in God and gives their allegiance to the Son of God, the Messiah, will have eternal life (Gen. 15:6; Dan. 12:1–2; Pss. 1:1, 6; 2:12).

Part 4: Intersection of the Narrative, Narrators, and Prophecies

1. From whatever angle you approach it, the Tanakh—when you let it communicate on its own terms instead of looking at it through the lens of some other teaching, such as the oral Torah—communicates a clear, vivid message. This has been illustrated by looking at the Narrative, the Narration, and Prophecies within the Tanakh.

Conclusion: The point of the Tanakh is that humans have sinned and are separated from their purpose, which involves dwelling with God. Instead, they are heading toward death. God decided to fix this by being born as a human child and dying in place of his humans. Everyone who trusts in what God did and gives their allegiance to the Son of God will be able to dwell with God, experiencing eternal life with Him.

5

The Tanakh and the New Testament

New Testament Authors See Their Story Rooted in the Tanakh

> He [Jesus] said to them, "These are My words which I spoke to you while I was still with you, that all the things that are written about Me in the Law of Moses and the Prophets and the Psalms must be fulfilled." (Luke 24:44)

Jesus—or Yeshua, as he would have been called while living in Israel—seemed to think that the whole Tanakh was about himself: "All the things that are written about Me in the Torah of Moses and the Prophets and the Psalms must be fulfilled" (Luke 24:44).

In ancient collections of scrolls, it was common to refer to the whole group by the title or author of the first book in that collection. The book of Psalms is the first book in the Writings section. So Yeshua was saying that everything written in the Torah, the Prophets, and the Writings—in other words, everything written in the Tanakh—is about him. We already saw that the Tanakh is about the Son of God, who would fulfill that King, Priest, Prophet role. When Yeshua claimed to be that person, it was a bold, yet coherent claim.

The words *testament* and *covenant* are synonyms. The difference is, *testament* comes from the Greek language, and *covenant* is a direct translation of the Hebrew word.[1] So the title "new testament/covenant" is a reference to the Tanakh prophet Jeremiah when he said:

> "Behold, days are coming," declares YHWH, "when I will make a new covenant with the house of Israel and the house of Judah, not like the covenant which I made with their fathers on the day I took them by the hand to bring them out of the land of Egypt, My covenant which they broke, although I was a husband to them," declares YHWH. "For this is the covenant which I will make with the house of Israel after those days," declares YHWH: "I will put My law within them and write it on their heart; and I will be their God, and they shall be My people. . . . for I will forgive their wrongdoing, and their sin I will no longer remember." (Jer. 31: 31–34)

Just as Yeshua saw himself as the fulfillment of everything written in the Tanakh, so did the New Testament authors. They intentionally linked their own writings to the Tanakh with the same literary connections that the Tanakh authors used to connect themselves together. One New Testament author, Mark, begins his account of Yeshua's life this way:

> The beginning of the gospel of Jesus Christ, the Son of God, just as it is written in Isaiah the prophet:
>
> "Behold, I am sending My messenger before You,
> Who will prepare Your way;
> The voice of one calling out in the wilderness,
> Prepare the way of the Lord,
> Make His paths straight!"
> John the Baptist appeared in the wilderness, preaching a baptism of repentance for the forgiveness of sins. (Mark 1:1–4)

The Tanakh and the New Testament

According to Mark, the gospel of Jesus Christ began a long time ago, in the Tanakh. Mark was linking his own writing to the Tanakh and describing the fulfillment of Isaiah's prophecies. He linked it by saying that John the baptizer announced Yeshua's ministry in the Spirit of Elijah, just like the Tanakh promised.

Another New Testament author, Matthew, began his scroll by presenting Yeshua's genealogy, starting with Abraham, the father of the Jewish people, and he closes the genealogy by saying that Yeshua is the Messiah (Matthew 1). By using a genealogy to open his work, Matthew is trying to express that Yeshua isn't a stand-alone story but is deeply rooted in the Tanakh.

A third New Testament author, John, began his scroll this way:

> In the beginning was the Word, and the Word was with God, and the Word was God. He was in the beginning with God. All things came into being through Him, and apart from Him not even one thing came into being that has come into being. In Him was life, and the life was the Light of mankind. And the Light shines in the darkness, and the darkness did not grasp it. (John 1:1–5)

Compare that with the opening lines of the Tanakh:

> In the beginning God created the heavens and the earth. And the earth was a formless and desolate emptiness, and darkness was over the surface of the deep, and the Spirit of God was hovering over the surface of the waters. Then God said, "Let there be light"; and there was light. God saw that the light was good; and God separated the light from the darkness. (Gen. 1:1–4)

John was trying to make it overly obvious that Yeshua is not new. He was there at the beginning of the Tanakh—the beginning of creation. Each of these gospel authors began his work by linking it to the Tanakh to show that the very thing the Tanakh was pointing to had arrived.

Yeshua's Life

The Sources

The primary sources on Yeshua's life are found in the New Testament. Other sources outside the New Testament function as corroboration for the reliability of the New Testament's documentation. Even without the New Testament sources, we have an outline of his life.[2] It's clear that the New Testament was written by people who believed Yeshua was the Messiah who the Tanakh is all about.[3] It's also clear they want other people to know Yeshua is the Messiah—they even tell us it's the reason they wrote their accounts. We can look to the other outside sources to confirm or falsify the New Testament accounts.[4]

We can be well assured that the apostles and their scribes were actually the people who wrote the New Testament because not only did the authors name themselves, but we have evidence from their contemporaries linking these books to their authors.[5] The books were copied and given to other early churches, who identified whom they received them from. This chain of custody was strong and accepted by the earliest contemporaries.[6] That raises a question: Why is the tradition for the authorship of these books reliable, but the rabbis' oral tradition is not and couldn't have come from Moses?

Here's why: The first evidence of anyone ever even discussing the oral Torah appeared over one thousand four hundred years after Moses would have received it at Mount Sinai. Whereas with the New Testament, we have attestations connecting the books to their authors within only a few years of the events they describe. Many of the people we have evidence from would have directly known people associated with the authors. We can be sure these apostles are in fact the authors of the New Testament. So we need to analyze how truthful and accurate their accounts are.

The authors intended us to think their books were accurate records, not entertaining fictional stories or legends. Their goal was that we really believe what they wrote (1 John 1:1–3). In order to make his readers more comfortable with the accuracy of his account, Luke packed his writing with references to historical people, places, and circumstances that are historically verifiable or falsifiable. Analyzing the second half of Luke's work, now called Acts of the Apostles, Professor Sherwin-White wrote, "For Acts the confirmation of historicity is overwhelming. Any attempt to reject its basic historicity even in matters of detail must now appear absurd."[69] It would have been even more immediately verifiable to those living in the area when Luke wrote it (Luke 3:1–3). We at least know that the New Testament authors weren't writing fiction. They intended their stories to be believed. Next, we have to determine if they could have been lying or mistaken.

The records contained inside the New Testament as well as from early enemies of Christians tell us that Yeshua's earliest followers were targets of persecution. Here's an example of this persecution recorded for us by the Jewish -non-Christian- Roman historian, Josephus. He was writing about James, one of the New Testament authors.

> He [Ananus] assembled the Sanhedrin of judges, and brought before them the brother of Jesus, who was called Christ [Messiah], whose name was James, and some others, (or, some of his companions); and when he had formed an accusation against them as breakers of the law, he delivered them to be stoned. (Josephus, *Antiquities* 20.9)

This example illustrates well the kind of persecution Christians faced. It doesn't stop there. The Roman emperor Nero used Christians as a scapegoat after the great fire in Rome. Pliny the Younger, one of the officers in charge of arresting and sentencing Christians, reports:

> In the meantime, this is the plan which I have adopted in the case of those Christians who have been brought before me. I ask them whether they are Christians; if they say yes, then I repeat the question a second and a third time, warning them of the penalties it entails, and if

they still persist, I order them to be taken away to prison. For I do not doubt that, whatever the character of the crime may be which they confess, their pertinacity and inflexible obstinacy certainly ought to be punished. (Pliny the Younger, book 10)

We further know that the authors of the New Testament thought they were telling the truth in writing their accounts. Many of the people they wrote to had also witnessed some of the events and would have been happy to point out any flaws. There's evidence that at least eight out of the twelve apostles went to their deaths for maintaining their claim that they had witnessed what they were telling people.[7] They didn't go to their death for simply believing it happened; they claimed they actually *saw* it. I don't know anyone who would die for a lie, especially not eight people for the same lie. They had no apparent motive. So we can be assured that the New Testament authors intended to convey accurate history.

We'll look into what they wrote about Yeshua's life. Then we'll see which events are corroborated by outside sources and what such confirmation tells us.

The New Testament consists of four eyewitness accounts of Yeshua's life, focusing on the final years leading up to his execution, during which he publicly taught how the kingdom of God was arriving, with him as its King. These records are called the Gospels, written by Matthew, Mark, Luke, and John.

Then there is a book called the Acts of the Apostles: a record of the early church, specifically the lives of Yeshua's closest students, known as apostles. The New Testament also includes twenty-one letters from these apostles to the earliest groups of Yeshua's followers, the first churches. Finally, the last book of the New Testament is an apocalyptic letter called the Revelation to John.

The apostle Paul wrote thirteen of the twenty-seven New Testament books. Paul was a Pharisee who studied under the well-known rabbi Gamaliel. Before Paul followed Yeshua and became one of the most prominent leaders in the Christian movement, he was the most vigorous persecutor of Christians. We have records that he hunted down Jewish people who were following Yeshua, to the point where he even stoned them.

Yeshua saw himself as the Messiah that the Tanakh was about. Furthermore, he saw himself as God, YHWH. The Tanakh lays out clear expectations for the Messiah that Yeshua would have to fit. As we've seen, according to the Tanakh, the Messiah must be the completely sinless Son of God who is God himself. He must be a prophet like Moses, teach the Torah, and atone for the people's sins so they can meet with God. He must be rejected by his generation, suffer, die, and rise from the dead.

We know, from the apostles' early letters to various churches and from outside sources, that the early followers of Yeshua believed he was the Messiah whom the Tanakh was about. Josephus, a Pharisee himself, recorded that early Christians believed Yeshua was the Christ. ("Christ" just means "Messiah" after being translated from Hebrew to Greek and then to English.) Both Josephus and another Roman non-Christian historian, Tacitus, record that the Romans crucified Yeshua after he was turned over to them by the Sanhedrin. Josephus, Tacitus, and a persecutor of the Christians named Pliny the Younger all record that the earliest Christians believed so strongly that Yeshua was who he said he was that they were ready to die instead of retracting their statements.

The Messiah Must Be the Son of God

When we let the Tanakh communicate on its own terms, we see it is clearly all about one person who will come through a specific genealogy, and that person becomes known as the Messiah. The Tanakh describes what the Messiah will do and what he'll be like.

Yeshua claimed to be the Messiah written about in the Tanakh, so we are analyzing his life in light of the Tanakh's expectations for the Messiah. There are many such expectations. We uncovered that he must be the Son of God whom God would install as his King:

> "As for Me, I have installed My King
> Upon Zion, My holy mountain."
> "I will announce the decree of YHWH:
> He said to Me, 'You are My Son,
> Today I have fathered You.'"
>
> (Ps. 2:6–7)

Matthew records an event that shows a fulfillment of those qualifications:

> After He was baptized, Jesus came up immediately from the water; and behold, the heavens were opened, and he saw the Spirit of God descending as a dove and settling on Him, and behold, a voice from the heavens said, "This is My beloved Son, with whom I am well pleased'" (Matt. 3:16–17)

The next qualification for the Messiah is that he function as a priest.

> YHWH has sworn and will not change His mind,
> "You are a priest forever
> According to the order of Melchizedek."
>
> (Ps. 110:4)

Yeshua acted as a priest doing things similar to that of the temple priests, but in an amplified way. Priests would make atonement so sins could be forgiven (Lev. 4:20). Yeshua forgave sins (Mark 2:5-11). Priests would inspect and determine if someone was clean to enter the holy temple (Lev. 13:3). Yeshua healed the unclean and restored them so they could enter the holy temple (Matt. 8:2-3). Another role priests performed was teaching the Torah.

The New Testament is filled with accounts of Yeshua teaching from the Torah and calling the people to turn away from their sin and trust in God. One of Yeshua's well-known teachings about the Torah is called the Sermon on the Mount. In it, he said:

> "Do not presume that I came to abolish the Law or the Prophets; I did not come to abolish, but to fulfill. For truly I say to you, until heaven and earth pass away, not the smallest letter or stroke of a letter shall pass from the Law, until all is accomplished!" (Matt. 5:17–18)

He's saying he didn't come to get rid of or replace the Tanakh (Torah, Prophets, and Writings). He came as the person whom the whole Tanakh was about. Yeshua taught that he fulfilled the expectations the Tanakh outlined for the Messiah. As the fulfillment of the Tanakh, Yeshua didn't come to get rid of it; he came to teach the right interpretation of it. Yeshua actually showed that the Tanakh had a higher standard than the people thought. He'd frequently say things along the lines of, "You may have heard it this way, but I'm telling you that *this* is what the Torah means"—usually referencing an oral tradition. By saying, "You've heard this, but I tell you this," he implied that he saw his authority as equal to the Torah's. Since the Torah's authority is God's authority, Jesus was implying that he is God.

> "You have heard that it was said, 'You shall not commit adultery'; but I say to you that everyone who looks at a woman with lust for her has already committed adultery with her in his heart. Now if your right eye is causing you to sin, tear it out and throw it away from you." (Matt. 5:27–29)

I'd also like to point out to the reader the direct contrast between the way Yeshua saw women and the oral Torah's view of women. Yeshua taught that if a man even looks at a woman intending to use her to satisfy his own sexual desire instead of giving himself to her in love, he alone is accountable (Matt. 5:28). The oral Torah teaches otherwise:

> A woman is a flask full of feces, and her mouth is full of blood. (Shabbat 152a)

A man's wife is permitted to him. Therefore, a man may do whatever he desires with his wife. He may engage in relations whenever he desires." (Mishnah Torah Issurei Biah 21:9)

The Messiah Must Be Without Sin

One important credential of the promised Messiah was that he be sinless. The Messiah had to be righteous before God.

> By His knowledge the Righteous One,
> My Servant, will justify the many,
> For He will bear their wrongdoings.
>
> (Isa. 53:11)

> You will not abandon my soul to Sheol;
> You will not allow Your Holy One to undergo decay.
>
> (Ps. 16:10)

The gospel authors tell us that the same deceiver who convinced Adam and Eve to doubt God tempted Yeshua as well. The deceiver took God's words and twisted them to deceive the couple into doubting God, and he employed the same method with Yeshua.

> He said to the woman, "Has God really said, 'You shall not eat from any tree of the garden'? The woman said to the serpent, "From the fruit of the trees of the garden we may eat; but from the fruit of the tree which is in the middle of the garden, God has said, 'You shall not eat from it or touch it, or you will die.'" The serpent said to the woman, "You certainly will not die! For God knows that on the day you eat from it your eyes will be opened, and you will become like God, knowing good and evil."

> When the woman saw that the tree was good for food,

and that it was a delight to the eyes, and that the tree was desirable to make one wise, she took some of its fruit and ate; and she also gave some to her husband with her, and he ate." (Gen. 3:1–6)

Adam and Eve gave in. But when the deceiver used the same tactic with Yeshua, tempting him by twisting God's words, Yeshua didn't give in:

"If You are the Son of God, command that these stones become bread." But He answered and said, "It is written: 'Man shall not live on bread alone, but on every word that comes out of the mouth of God.'"

Then the devil took Him along into the holy city and had Him stand on the pinnacle of the temple, and he said to Him, "If You are the Son of God, throw Yourself down; for it is written:

'He will give His angels orders concerning You';
and
'On their hands they will lift You up,
So that You do not strike
Your foot against a stone.'"

Jesus said to him, "On the other hand, it is written: 'You shall not put the Lord your God to the test.'"

Again, the devil took Him along to a very high mountain and showed Him all the kingdoms of the world and their glory; and he said to Him, "All these things I will give You, if You fall down and worship me." Then Jesus said to him, "Go away, Satan! For it is written: 'You shall worship the Lord your God, and serve Him only.'"

Then the devil left Him; and behold, angels came and began to serve Him. (Matt. 4:3–11)

Later on, in the garden of Gethsemane the night before his crucifixion, Jesus has another moment when he resists taking what he wants and accepts what God says is good. Knowing He will be tried and crucified the next day, he is a little stressed out. Actually, he's so stressed out that the Bible depicts him experiencing what seems to be a panic attack.

According to the Bible, Yeshua had been one with the Father for all eternity, even before creation. But now He's going to "bear their wrongdoings" (Isa. 53:11). By bearing the punishment for sin, he's not only going to experience death, but he's also going to be separated from his Father. The gospel author Luke records that Yeshua was so upset he began to sweat blood. That might have seemed like hyperbole to readers at the time, but we now know that under times of extreme anxiety, sweating blood is a real medical experience called *hematidrosis*.[8]

Yet despite his severe anxiety, Yeshua didn't waiver from what God the Father wanted for him. He labeled the fear as a moment of desire and told the Father, essentially, "Even though I want you to remove this from me, I want what you want more":

> "Father, if You are willing, remove this cup from Me; yet not My will, but Yours be done." [Now an angel from heaven appeared to Him, strengthening Him. And being in agony, He was praying very fervently; and His sweat became like drops of blood, falling down upon the ground]. (Luke 22:42–44)

Adam and Eve, confronted by a moment of desire in a garden, gave in, bringing a curse on all creation. Abraham was the first step in undoing that curse. Abraham's descendant Yeshua, the woman's offspring, is depicted in a different garden confronted with his own moment of desire, but he does *not* give in to it.

This took place in a garden to show us that Yeshua's sinlessness is not just a nice quality about him; it's essential to reversing the curse. Yeshua's sinlessness brings blessing to the world. The New Testament authors emphasize its importance:

> You know that He appeared in order to take away sins; and in Him there is no sin. (1 John 3:5)

> We do not have a high priest who cannot sympathize with our weaknesses, but One who has been tempted in all things just as we are, yet without sin. (Heb. 4:15)

The Messiah Must Suffer and Die

The Tanakh teaches that the Messiah must be rejected by his generation, suffer, and then die in place of his people.

> He poured out His life unto death,
> And was counted with wrongdoers;
> Yet He Himself bore the sin of many,
> And interceded for the wrongdoers.
>
> (Isa. 53:12)

There's overwhelming evidence that Yeshua was crucified and died. No modern historian argues otherwise. The New Testament has four detailed accounts by different authors that corroborate each other. His crucifixion and death are discussed in all twenty-seven New Testament books. The New Testament authors record that the Sanhedrin rejected Yeshua, arrested him, and turned him over to a Roman named Pontius Pilate. Pontius Pilate had him flogged and then crucified. The Roman historian Tacitus confirmed Yeshua's crucifixion and added that it was the most extreme punishment a person could experience.

> Nero fastened the guilt and inflicted the most exquisite tortures on a class hated for their abominations, called Christians by the populace. Christus, from whom the name had its origin, suffered the extreme penalty during the reign of Tiberius at the hands of one of our procurators, Pontius Pilatus, and a most mischievous superstition,

thus checked for the moment, again broke out not only in
Judea. (Tacitus Annals 15.44)

Yeshua spoke about his death even before his trials. He explained that he came to earth to die. *It's why he came.*

> He began to teach them that the Son of Man must suffer many things and be rejected by the elders and the chief priests and the scribes, and be killed, and after three days rise from the dead. And He was stating the matter plainly. And Peter took Him aside and began to rebuke Him. But turning around and seeing His disciples, He rebuked Peter and said, "Get behind Me, Satan; for you are not setting your mind on God's purposes, but on man's." (Mark 8:31–33, cf. Matt. 17:22-23, Luke 18:31-32)

The Son of Man is the term that Yeshua used most often for himself, and it's a reference to Daniel's prophecy about a future human ruler sitting on the divine throne (Dan. 7:13). Yeshua taught that his purpose for coming to earth was actually to be rejected, suffer, die and rise from the dead. His death was so important that when one of his closest disciples, Peter, didn't like the plan, Yeshua called him by the name of the deceiver from Genesis 3 that he had come to defeat.

Yeshua saw his death as the fulfillment of everything written in the Tanakh: "All the things that have been written through the prophets about the Son of Man will be accomplished" (Luke 18:31). He spoke those words in reference to his rejection, suffering, death, and resurrection. Yeshua's closest disciples didn't understand that the Tanakh was all about his death, until three days after he died. Before that, they missed it just like so many of our people miss it today. But Yeshua held firm that his death would be the fulfillment of everything written in Scriptures.

The Messiah's Death Won't Be the End for Him

The Tanakh teaches that the Messiah would be born as a baby on earth, that he would be the son of God, be God himself, and die to pay the punishment that everyone else deserves. It also teaches that his death would not be permanent. The Prophecies tell us that after he gave up his life and died, God would give him plunder and a portion with "the great."

> He will bear their wrongdoings.
> Therefore, I will allot Him a portion with the great,
> And He will divide the plunder with the strong,
> Because He poured out His life unto death.
>
> (Isa. 53:11–12)

We have seen that he will be God's King and reign forever, so the prophet must be talking about when he will inherit that kingdom. Since you can't reign forever if you're dead, this sets up an expectation that after the Messiah died, he would be raised from the dead and reign forever.

So, looking at Yeshua's life to see if he meets the standards for the Messiah, we need to know: Was he really raised from the dead? It's obvious Christians today think he was—but was he?

When I was twenty-one, I went to Israel with a small group. One day I left the group and started wandering around Jerusalem by myself. I found myself in the Christian quarter of Jerusalem near a church where many people were standing around a stone slab, weeping and kissing the stone. I was confused for a moment until something wild occurred to me. I walked up to a woman who looked like another American tourist and asked her, "Is that where Jesus was crucified?"

It turned out it wasn't where he was crucified and the woman was not an American tourist, or apparently from anywhere that speaks English. She turned to me and, in the most broken English I have ever heard, said, "Jesus died . . . three days . . . rise again . . . believe!"

This woman, who could barely speak any English, could still communicate to me that Yeshua died and then rose again. It's clear that Christians today think he rose from the dead—but did the first Christians think that? Could they have believed something else that later developed into a legend of his resurrection? More importantly, even if they did think he rose from the dead, can a person today have enough evidence to believe it beyond any reasonable doubt?

The New Testament authors are clear they fully believed—based on their own eyeballs—that Yeshua rose from the dead. His resurrection is mentioned in all twenty-seven New Testament books, multiple times in each book. All the New Testament books are either written by people who either claimed to have actually seen Yeshua alive after he died or whose writing was directly supervised by someone who had seen the resurrected Yeshua. In fact, after Judas turned Yeshua over to the Sanhedrin, the apostles had to choose a replacement. The most important credential to them was that it was someone who was around before Yeshua died and then saw him again alive after he died.

> "It is necessary that of the men who have accompanied us all the time that the Lord Jesus went in and out among us—beginning with the baptism of John until the day that He was taken up from us—one of these must become a witness with us of His resurrection." (Acts 1: 21-22)

Each of the four detailed accounts of Yeshua's life in the New Testament have minor differences. These minor differences are never about essential details. We have to keep in mind that these books are intended to be a form of communication. The Gospels, according to Matthew, Mark, Luke, and John, are eyewitness accounts of Yeshua's life, death, and resurrection. So, when we read through an eyewitness account and compare it to another eyewitness account, there *should* be some differences. Every person is going to experience the same event a little bit differently.

Ask a married couple how they met and they'll tell you the same story, but usually with different details. The things each person notices, the things that don't stand out to them, and the minor background details are going to be remembered slightly differently. The justice system today actually finds witnesses more credible if their testimonies vary a bit on minor details from the other witness. If the stories of two people—or four, in the case of the Gospels—line up exactly on every detail, it's likely that they discussed their stories beforehand and changed the details to suit their shared agenda instead of giving an honest account. That's not what we see in the New Testament accounts of Yeshua's resurrection. Instead, their stories all line up on the major details, while on background details that could have been perceived differently, there are minor differences.

The Gospels give us four detailed accounts of Yeshua's death and resurrection, but the New Testament authors also talk about the resurrection elsewhere. In his first letter to the Corinthian church, Paul quoted a creed he had been taught about Yeshua. We know what he's passing along is a creed because of how he announces it: "For I handed down to you . . . what I also received" (1Cor. 15:3). Moreover, its content condenses the most important beliefs of the early church into a short poem for memory. And that's what a creed is: just an oral tradition organized into a fixed form by the systematic linguistic tools we talked about in chapter 3. When did Paul get this creed? Well, Yeshua was crucified in 30 CE at the earliest, and Paul began to follow Yeshua about two years later.[9] Paul was immediately surrounded by a church at that time, and he met with the other apostles about three years later, which would be 35 CE. So, within five years of Yeshua's death, Paul was taught an organized oral tradition in its finalized form about what the earliest followers of Yeshua believed. Since Paul learned it and didn't write it himself the creed must have been created even earlier. Some scholars think it goes back to within months of the crucifixion! This is what it said:[10]

> I handed down to you as of first importance what I also received, that Christ died for our sins according to the Scriptures, and that He was buried, and that He was raised on the third day according to the Scriptures, and that He appeared to Cephas, then to the twelve. After that He appeared to more than five hundred brothers and sisters at one time, most of whom remain until now, but some have fallen asleep; then He appeared to James, then to all the apostles; [then Paul adds to the tradition] and last of all, as to one untimely born, He appeared to me

also. (1 Cor. 15: 3–8)

Five years, let alone a few months, is definitely not enough time for a legend to develop and replace a solid set of historical facts. Here we see that the early church believed Yeshua was the Christ [Messiah], and that he died and was raised again. Yeshua's earliest followers were convinced that Yeshua was raised from the dead. But did they have sufficient evidence for that belief? Do we?

We should note that during Yeshua's lifetime Jerusalem was a small but populous city. Yeshua quickly became a very popular figure throughout Israel, but especially in Jerusalem. Even the Talmud admits that Yeshua was going around performing miracles (along with his students). The sages try to explain Yeshua's miracles away by saying he was performing sorcery: "And the Master says: Jesus performed sorcery, incited Jews to engage in idolatry, and led Israel astray." (Sanhedrin 107b)

It isn't hard to imagine that, as a Jewish teacher traveling around Israel performing miracles, Yeshua would amass big crowds. That's exactly what the sources record. Tacitus and Josephus both state that Yeshua was a popular figure who had huge crowds following him—sometimes more than five thousand people, according to the New Testament writers.

The sources tell us Yeshua was a public figure who was crucified in a small city—at least in its physical size, Jerusalem was not large. It wouldn't be a long walk from one side to the other. I've walked that distance myself, from one side to the other and back, and I had time for sightseeing on the way. The whole trip took me only about three hours, including a few stops and detours. But however you interpret the evidence, it's undeniable that in this small city on the week of Passover about two thousand years ago, something happened that changed the course of human history.

We're going to analyze the significance of the evidence we have for what actually happened during that unforgettable week. We'll look at the evidence concerning Yeshua's famous entry into Jerusalem, his immediate arrest, trials, torture, and execution that followed. We'll then examine the evidence about who knew the location of his tomb. Finally, we'll analyze the validity of claims from people in that same small city that Yeshua had come back to life.

Yeshua was a Public Figure

The Torah commands Jewish men to travel to the temple in Jerusalem every year for three feasts: Passover, Shavuot, and Sukkot. Yeshua was crucified on Passover, a time when Jewish men from all over would have been traveling to the small city of Jerusalem for the festival. The four detailed eyewitness accounts each record that Yeshua was killed on Passover, and the Talmud admits it as well (Sanhedrin 43a). Yeshua was crucified with the backdrop of an overcrowded Jerusalem.

About four days before Passover, Yeshua famously entered the city on a donkey while the crowds cheered and called out, "Hosanna!" which means, "Please save!" He chose to enter on a donkey to fulfill Zechariah's prophecy about the Messiah.

> Rejoice greatly, daughter of Zion!
> Shout *in triumph*, daughter of Jerusalem!
> Behold, your king is coming to you;
> He is righteous and endowed with salvation,
> Humble, and mounted on a donkey,
> Even on a colt, the foal of a donkey.
>
> (Zech. 9:9)

[As they approached Jerusalem,] the disciples went and did just as Jesus had instructed them, and brought the donkey and the colt, and laid their cloaks on them; and He sat on the cloaks. Most of the crowd spread their cloaks on the road, and others were cutting branches from the trees and spreading them on the road. Now the crowds going ahead of Him, and those who followed, were shouting,

"Hosanna to the Son of David;

Blessed is the One who comes in the name of the Lord;

> Hosanna in the highest!"
>
> When He had entered Jerusalem, all the city was stirred, saying, "Who is this?" (Matt. 21:6–10)

Most of the people cheering for Yeshua, if not all of them, thought he was the Messiah. But, led astray by oral traditions or some other misinterpretation, they thought messiahship meant he would free them from their current Roman oppression, not save them from evil—from their own sin.

Those that didn't think Yeshua was the Messiah thought he was a prophet, still a big deal. So, we know that Yeshua entered Jerusalem a few days before the Passover, when he was killed, and was greeted by crowds of people cheering for him. Yeshua was a celebrity entering a small city where everyone was fully aware of his presence. Word spreads fast, especially when people think the Messiah they've been waiting for since Moses has arrived.

Arrest and Trials

Only about four days after Yeshua entered the city amid the cheering crowds, he was arrested by the temple priests and elders, tried by the Sanhedrin, brought before two different gentile courts, and then crucified.

We have four separate eyewitness accounts of Yeshua's arrest in the accounts of Matthew, Mark, Luke, and John. In those four independent reports, after celebrating the Passover dinner, one of Yeshua's core twelve disciples turned him over to the temple leaders, who had been looking for a reason to prosecute him. The priests interrogated him, then sentenced him to death. But since, under Roman authority, Jews weren't allowed to perform their own executions, they turned him over to the Roman ruler Pontius Pilate.

> Early in the morning the chief priests with the elders, scribes, and the entire Council immediately held a consultation; and they bound Jesus and led Him away,

and turned Him over to Pilate. . . .

And the crowd went up and began asking Pilate to do as he had been accustomed to do for them. Pilate answered them, saying, 'Do you want me to release for you the King of the Jews?' For he was aware that the chief priests had handed Him over because of envy. But the chief priests stirred up the crowd to ask him to release Barabbas for them instead. And responding again, Pilate said to them, "Then what shall I do with Him whom you call the King of the Jews?" They shouted back, "Crucify Him!" (Mark 15:1, 8–13)

So, Yeshua was arrested by the temple leaders, who interrogated him and decided he deserved to die. Then they turned him over to the Romans to crucify him, which is when the public got involved. Pilate offered to free Yeshua, but the crowds all called for a different prisoner to be released instead. All four detailed accounts show that the crowds were fully aware of Yeshua's crucifixion. Everyone knew Yeshua was in town, and the public quickly turned from thinking he was the Messiah to calling for his crucifixion, one of the most painful deaths ever invented.

Execution

Crucifixion was invented by the Persians but was then perfected by the Romans as a method of execution so cruel it could only legally be performed on a foreigner. Before Yeshua was crucified, he was flogged, which is similar to being whipped except with leather straps with bits of metal shards and balls attached. The metal would rip into your flesh and pull it out, often exposing the veins and bones underneath.

After flogging Yeshua, the Romans nailed his wrists and feet to the cross. For a crucifixion victim, death came by suffocation. Hanging by his hands, the person could breathe in, but to breathe out, he had to push up on the nails in his feet, with his open back wounds rubbing against the wood. Eventually, he wouldn't be able to push up anymore, and he would suffocate. Sometimes the process took days.

All four detailed independent accounts of Yeshua's life in the New Testament record Yeshua's execution by crucifixion. All twenty-seven books in the New Testament—again, all written by eyewitnesses—discuss Yeshua's crucifixion. The extrabiblical records from Josephus, Tacitus, and Pliny the Younger all mention his execution, most specifying crucifixion.

The Talmud stands alone in denying the crucifixion. Why? Because his crucifixion shows that the Jewish leaders who sentenced Yeshua were not motivated by Torah observance. According to the Tanakh, the only acceptable method of execution was stoning. Stoning is the only execution ever prescribed in the Tanakh (Lev. 20:2, 27; 24:16; Num. 15:35; Deut. 13:11; 17:5; 21:21; 22:21, and more). Other modes of execution are mentioned in the Tanakh, but only for very rare and specific circumstances that clearly did not apply to Yeshua (Lev. 20:14; 21:9)

Burial Location

Most crucifixion victims were buried in a common criminal tomb, but this wasn't required, and occasionally their friends or family would bury them in a personal tomb. The accounts of Yeshua's death record him being buried in the tomb of a man named Joseph of Arimathea, a member of the Sanhedrin. Unlike the majority of the Sanhedrin, Joseph believed Yeshua was the Messiah.

The fact that the tomb belonged to a specific member of the Sanhedrin is a crucial detail, because Yeshua's followers wrote these accounts. They did their best to record these stories truthfully. But had they been lying, this would have been a foolish, self-destructive lie. A false account of Yeshua's burial that identified the tomb's owner as a member of the very group that ordered Yeshua's crucifixion would have collapsed in on itself. Everyone could go and ask the Sanhedrin for Joseph of Arimathea's tomb's location. The lie would be instantly falsifiable. That is probably why the Sanhedrin never claimed Yeshua's disciples were lying about the empty tomb. Instead, they confirmed the tomb was empty and tried to explain it by claiming the disciples stole the body.

So, eyewitnesses recorded Yeshua's specific burial location in writing. But can we also be sure people in Jerusalem at the time would have known where Yeshua was buried? Well, yes. Remember Paul's creed that we discussed—the one that goes back to within a few years of the cross at the latest, and most likely was finalized just a few months after the cross. That creed confirms all the basic information recorded in all four gospels, namely Yeshua's death, *burial,* and resurrection. While the creed doesn't acknowledge the specific location of the tomb, it records his burial as important and corroborates the accounts as a whole.

Furthermore, Mark wrote his account of all these things extremely early, so they could not be a later fabrication. Mark is considered the earliest written account because, instead of smooth, continuous narratives like the other gospels, his is written more like somebody's notes, neatened up enough to be published. Basically, Mark includes little, short details about Yeshua's life—except for the last week, with which Mark was primarily concerned. Writing about the end of Yeshua's life, Mark took the time to tell his narrative in greater detail, including the burial story.

All the evidence shows that Yeshua's burial location was public knowledge from the very beginning. Most New Testament scholars agree that the burial account of Yeshua is reliable. John A. T. Robinson, a New Testament scholar, captured this well when he said, "The Honorable burial of Jesus is one of the earliest and best-attested facts that we have about the historical Jesus."[11]

Imagine you were in Jerusalem for Passover in 30 CE and heard everyone saying that the Messiah had come to the city. You would probably be ecstatic—or at the very least, curious. But then, four days later, on Passover, he's crucified, a form of execution reserved for the worst criminals. At that point, you would probably be a little disappointed that he wasn't going to free you from Roman oppression anymore.

Three days later, though, the city is buzzing again. People start telling you that his followers have seen the dead man alive after his crucifixion. You don't believe this because you didn't know the Tanakh taught that the Messiah would die and rise again, but you decide to investigate. You might start by asking around for where Yeshua was buried and then go see for yourself if he was in the tomb. If Joseph of Arimathea didn't exist, you would know in about two seconds. If he was a real person and Yeshua wasn't really buried in Joseph's tomb, you would ask the Sanhedrin, and Joseph would be happy to tell you that the disciples made it up.

The only other option is that the disciples were telling the truth: Yeshua really was buried in Joseph of Arimathea's tomb. And if he's still in the grave, case closed. Yeshua isn't alive; he's dead in the tomb. Easy. But if he's not there . . .

Jerusalem was the one place where Yeshua's empty tomb was easily verifiable or falsifiable within a day. Had Yeshua still been in the tomb, Jerusalem would have been the last place we should expect to see Christianity explode. Yet Jerusalem is actually the *first* place where Christianity boomed. The New Testament author Luke, and Tacitus, an enemy of Christianity, both record that faith in Yeshua's resurrection first accelerated in Jerusalem (Acts 2:41; Tacitus Annals 15.44).

The temple leaders didn't even attempt to deny Yeshua's empty tomb. Instead, they confirmed it by claiming that the disciples stole his body. But we've already seen that the disciples' motive for faking his resurrection would be very weak. Their own suffering until death shows that they really believed they saw Yeshua alive after his crucifixion. Had these eyewitnesses renounced Yeshua, they would have been set free to return to their everyday lives (Pliny the Younger, book 10). Again, not many people would suffer and die for a lie, especially for absolutely no gain.

Why Did Yeshua's Generation Reject Him?

He was despised and abandoned by men,
A man of great pain and familiar with sickness;
And like one from whom people hide their faces,

He was despised, and we had no regard for Him.

(Isa. 53:3)

The Tanakh is clear about its message: God would send his Son to deal with the evil that invaded creation when humans decided to sin. His Son is called the Messiah, and we know he would be born as a baby and go on to suffer, die, and rise again.

But we know he would suffer and die because his generation would reject him: "And as for His generation, who considered that He was cut off from the land of the living For the wrongdoing of my people, to whom the blow was due?" (Isa. 53:8). Prophecy explicitly teaches that the Messiah would be rejected and pierced when he came. It also teaches this in the narrative by a repeating pattern. Most of the prophets were rejected by Israel's leaders; many of them were even killed. Even Moses was rejected the first time he tried to save Israel. It wasn't until he came back to save them the second time that they followed him (Ex. 2:14; 4:29–31). The sons of Israel (Jacob) didn't recognize Joseph the first time they came for help. They only recognized him the second time (Gen. 42:8; 45:1-5). The Messiah's rejection is explicitly prophesied, and because it is also a well-developed pattern, we should expect it even if it wasn't prophesied about him.

But why exactly did Yeshua's generation reject him? What was their charge against him? To put it simply, they sentenced Yeshua to death because he claimed to be God.

Many people think, "Even though Yeshua's followers clearly thought he was God, Yeshua never actually claimed to be God." And in a sense they'd be right because Yeshua never used the words "I am God." But in a more real sense, they'd be wrong because Yeshua *did* claim to be God many times.

In the account of Yeshua's life as recorded by John, Yeshua made multiple "I am" statements. What does that have to do with anything?

You might be familiar with the story of the burning bush, where God revealed his sacred name to Moses. Moses asked God what His name is, and God said, "EHYH ASER EHYH," which literally means "I am that I am"—or, more easily understood in English, "I am He that exists" (Ex. 3:14). But Moses is not the one that exists, so he doesn't go tell everyone, "I am He that exists." He tells the people, "He is He that exists." That is the Hebrew name you might be familiar with: "YHWH."

So, when Yeshua made these "I am" statements, he was claiming to be the eternal one who has always existed. He was claiming to be one with God:

> The Jews said to Him, "You are not yet fifty years old, and You have seen Abraham?" Jesus said to them, "Truly, truly I say to you, before Abraham was born, I am." (John 8:57)

Yeshua had just claimed that Abraham had seen him, and they asked how a young man could have seen Abraham, who lived thousands of years ago. Yeshua answered by saying, "I am."

About two hundred years before Yeshua, the Jewish scribes translated the Tanakh into Greek so that Jews would be able to read Scripture despite the growing Greek influence. This translation was called the *Septuagint*.[12] The New Testament was also written in Greek. The Jewish scholars who translated the Tanakh into Greek used the exact words for God's name when He told it to Moses that John recorded Yeshua applying to himself. Everyone who heard his statement would have known he was calling himself the name of God. In fact, they did understand that he was calling himself YHWH, and it made them so angry they wanted to kill him (John 8:59).

Yeshua used a term for himself that always seemed to make the religious leaders, specifically many Pharisees, angry. This title was "the Son of Man," it was by far the most common way Yeshua referred to himself. This term upset the leaders because it was a title from a famous prophecy about a divine human.

> "I kept looking in the night visions,
> And behold, with the clouds of heaven
> One like a son of man was coming,
> And He came up to the Ancient of Days
> And was presented before Him.

> And to Him was given dominion,
> Honor, and a kingdom,
> So that all the peoples, nations, and populations of all languages
> Might serve Him.
> His dominion is an everlasting dominion
> Which will not pass away;
> And His kingdom is one
> Which will not be destroyed."
>
> (Dan. 7:13–14)

This prophecy is about a human-like person given all the glory and authority that only belongs to God. Jewish interpretations of this prophecy preceding Yeshua taught that it was about a divine human figure who would rule on God's throne (1 Enoch 48: 2–6; 62:6–7). The Second Temple Period scroll of 4 Ezra also mentions the human-like being who existed before creation with the Most High, and the Most High referred to the human-like being as his Son. So it was a big deal for Yeshua to call himself the "Son of Man." By invoking the title Son of Man from Daniel 7 he was claiming to be one with God.

Yeshua didn't call himself *a* son of man; he called himself *the* Son of Man, making it clear he was not merely calling himself human. He was saying he was *the* human prophesied about in Daniel. This prophecy was well known, especially among the religious leaders questioning Yeshua. His claim made them angry.

Imagine talking to a superhero fan and calling yourself the Man of Steel. Immediately that superhero fan is going to know you are calling yourself Superman. This is what Yeshua was doing. He used a well-known term the Pharisees and priests were very familiar with and applied it to himself.

We have plenty of evidence that this title infuriated the Jewish leaders, but it reached a climax at Yeshua's trial before the Sanhedrin. Three detailed independent accounts record this for us. We'll look at Mark's.

> The high priest stood up and came forward and questioned Jesus, saying, "Do You not offer any answer for what these men are testifying against You?" But He kept silent and did not offer any answer. Again the high priest was questioning Him, and said to Him, "Are You the Christ, the Son of the Blessed One?" And Jesus said, "I am; and you shall see the Son of Man sitting at the right hand of power, and coming with the clouds of heaven." Tearing his clothes, the high priest said, "What further need do we have of witnesses? You have heard the blasphemy; how does it seem to you?" And they all condemned Him as deserving of death." (Mark 14:60–64)

All at once, Yeshua not only answered that he was the Messiah, but he added that as the Messiah, he was the divine-human Son of God from Daniel 7, equal to God. The high priest and all the Jewish leaders present took this as ultimate blasphemy because Yeshua was here using loaded language to say he was one with God. You can imagine a geeky little kid being questioned in a comic bookstore: "Do you really think you are Superman?" And the kid says, "I am, and you'll see the Man of Steel shooting lasers out of his eyes." When Yeshua told his accusers he was the Messiah and the divine Son of God, they condemned him to death.

Even though the Tanakh teaches that the Messiah is the Son of God who is one with God (cf. Ps. 2: 4–12; Isa. 53: 5; Zech. 12:10). The religious leaders of the day were already being heavily influenced by the oral traditions of the Pharisees. Much of the oral Torah developed after Yeshua, but it was first introduced in 150 BCE. So, the idea of an oral Torah had already been around for about 180 years by the time Yeshua claimed to be the Son of Man. And the oral Torah doesn't portray the Messiah as divine; just as a man who will rule on earth and establish earthly peace.

The religious leaders therefore totally missed the point of the Messiah. They didn't realize he came to fulfill God's promise to Eve, to deliver a fatal blow to the snake while receiving a deadly blow himself

(Gen. 3:15). They thought his mission was solely to establish worldly peace. They didn't realize he first needed to deal with their sins so he could establish peace between God and men. Yet resolving the conflict caused by human sin is the very centerpiece of the messianic mission.

The Jewish leaders didn't understand what the Messiah was supposed to do, so they didn't recognize him, which should be no surprise. "As for His generation, who considered that He was cut off from the land of the living For the wrongdoing of my people to whom the blow was due?."

According to all the records, the historical Yeshua fits the Tanakh's description of the Messiah perfectly. Even though most sages of Israel rejected Yeshua as the Messiah, thousands of Jewish people did recognize him and began to follow him.

The Tanakh taught that the Messiah must be one with God. Yet he would be born as a human child who God calls his own Son, and that his generation would reject him. The Tanakh teaches that he'll suffer, die, and rise again (cf. Isa. 53; Ps. 16:8–11). All the evidence shows that the historical Yeshua amazingly fits all these descriptions.

If we want to do things the Jewish way and embrace our Jewish identity, we have a choice to make. Just like a tree represented Adam and Eve's choice, our choice is also represented by a tree, this time in the form of a cross. Yeshua taught that he was the Messiah, the one who the Tanakh wrote about, and we have sufficient evidence that he meets all the criteria set forward for the Messiah in the Tanakh. So Yeshua must be the Messiah. The least Jewish thing a Jewish person can do is reject the Jewish Messiah. The Jewish Way must be to accept and follow the Messiah—the Prophet, High Priest, and King of the Jewish people.

Yeshua's Messianic Mission: The Gospel

Let's recall what we know the Tanakh was about. We looked first at its narrative, which teaches that God designed a good world where he provided good things in abundance. As the Being from which every other good thing in existence came, God knows what is good and what is not. He designed humans to dwell with him—to live in relationship with God. But humans tried to be like God and decide for themselves what was good, so they violated God's command by taking what they thought looked good , bringing sin into creation.

Thus sin entered the world. But the narrative in the Tanakh showed us that God immediately had a plan to deal with sin: He would use the offspring of Eve, Abraham, Judah, and David to undo the curses that came about because of sin. The narrators of the Tanakh showed us that the entire Tanakh is entirely about this Messiah-Prophet figure, and that anyone who won't listen to him will be cut off from the people (Deut. 18:19).

The Prophets then reveal even more specifics about God's plan: for God Himself to be the Messiah, who would

- come to earth as a baby: "A child will be born to us, a son will be given to us; and the government will rest on His shoulders" (Isa. 9:6).
- pay the punishment for our sins by dying: "He poured out His life unto death" (Isa. 53:12).
- be resurrected by God the Father: "If He renders Himself as a guilt offering, He will see His offspring, He will prolong His days" (Isa. 53:10).

However, the Prophets did not teach that *everyone* would be saved after the Messiah died for our sins and was resurrected. Only some will have everlasting life: "Those who sleep in the dust of the ground will awake, these [whose names are in God's book] to everlasting life, but the others to disgrace and everlasting contempt" (Dan. 12:2). Those who give their allegiance to God's Son, the Messiah, will have everlasting life. The rest will perish. "Kiss the Son, that He not be angry and you perish on the way" (Ps. 2:12).

The entire Tanakh teaches that everyone has sinned, and the punishment for sin is death and separation from God. That puts *everyone* in a very unfortunate position. But from the very beginning, God loved his creation so much that he had a plan to redeem it. He decided to send His Son, who is one with Himself, to die and pay the punishment of sin so we wouldn't have to. Anyone who would then turn and give their allegiance to His Son will have everlasting life.

For anyone who refuses to accept God's gift of life, God will honor that choice and keep them separated from himself. But separate from him, there is no good because every good thing is provided only by God.

In the biblical story, God pleads with people repeatedly that everyone would turn and experience the good things he wants to give them: "YHWH, God of their fathers, sent word to them again and again by His messengers, because He had compassion on His people and on His dwelling place" (2 Chron. 36:15). The Tanakh, then, is a loving message from a Father who loves his people deeply and sincerely wants them to turn to him

> "How I would set you among My sons
> And give you a pleasant land,
> The most beautiful inheritance of the nations!'
> And I said, 'You shall call Me, My Father,
> And not turn away from following Me.'"
>
> (Jer. 3:19)

Writing to a younger Jewish follower of Yeshua named Timothy, the apostle Paul summarized the teachings of the Tanakh well: "From childhood you have known the sacred writings which are able to give you the wisdom that leads to salvation through faith which is in Christ Jesus" (2 Tim. 3:14).

Paul held that the entire Tanakh was about the Messiah. Originally a violently opposed skeptic, he became convinced, based on evidence from his own eyes, that Yeshua was that Messiah. The only sacred writings Timothy would have known from childhood were the Tanakh. So, rephrasing Paul's statement, biblical scholar Tim Mackie said, "The Tanakh is able to make you aware that you need to be rescued by trusting the Messiah, Jesus.[13]"

How can we trust God's version of good and evil when our own way seems right to us? First, we can be sure that God takes evil far more seriously than we do. When God created the world, he saw that it was good, and throughout the Tanakh, we see time and time again that God deeply loves and cares about his creation. And specifically, he has *our* best interests in mind. He loved us so much that he actually died for us while we were still rejecting him.

God doesn't hate evil only because people are rebelling against him; he also hates evil because it causes pain and suffering in the good world he loves. There are terrible things in the world that we all hate and want gone. I'm sure you hate the idea of children being physically abused and murdered, and you want that gone from the world. Yeshua tells us that God takes it far more seriously than you and me (Matt. 5). He doesn't just want child murder gone from the world; he wants anger gone from his creation. He doesn't just want rape gone from his good world; he wants lust gone; he wants the desire to use someone else for our own sexual pleasure, instead of giving ourselves to them in love, gone from his world.

He takes evil much more seriously than we do, and he's telling us we can and should trust him. So, we can see that God's plan to overcome sin is also a mission to remove pain and suffering from the world. "He will wipe away every tear from their eyes; and there will no longer be any death; there will no longer be any mourning, or crying, or pain; the first things have passed away" (Rev. 21:4).

But when we look at where evil starts, we may realize, "Wait—God wants anger gone from the world? And he wants even the desire to use someone else for our own sexual pleasure gone for the world? That's unsettling. *I've* done those things. I've been angry. I've had lustful thoughts. Even though I might not have killed another person, or sexually abused someone, I'm still part of the problem. I'm bringing evil into God's good creation."

So, if we wonder why God doesn't just wipe out evil right now so people stop suffering, there's this reality: If he did wipe out evil right now, we'd be gone too. Our own anger, lust, jealousy, and other similar selfish intentions are the source of evil in the world. We want evil gone from the world—but we don't want to be gone.

Here's the good news: When I trust Yeshua's definition of good and evil, he will get rid of the evil in me (cf. Rom. 12:2; Phil. 1:6). Even though we are corrupting his creation with these self-focused desires, his plan wasn't to simply come and destroy us. From the beginning, he announced a plan to rid evil from the world *and* heal us. "The punishment for our well-being was laid upon Him, and by His wounds we are healed" (Isa. 53:5).

Yeshua appeared and announced his mission using the word *gospel*. According to the detailed accounts of Yeshua's life, he went around preaching "the gospel." He told people to repent and believe the gospel. But what is the gospel?

The Greek word for "gospel," *euangelion*, was a term packed with context. It literally meant "good news," but it was specifically used in royal announcements of a new king. So, when Yeshua and his followers said, "Repent and believe the gospel," they were saying, "Turn from your old leader—yourself—and believe or trust in the new King." Yeshua was saying that the kingdom of God was arriving because the King had arrived.

Here is what Yeshua said about the good news:

> Jesus came into Galilee, preaching the gospel of God, and saying, "The time is fulfilled, and the kingdom of God is at hand; repent and believe in the gospel." (Mark 1:14–15)

Mark wrote that Yeshua was preaching the gospel of God. What exactly did Yeshua preach? He said, "The time is fulfilled, and the kingdom of God is at hand," and Mark called that statement the gospel of God. Yeshua was teaching that the kingdom of God (or the kingdom of heaven—he used the two terms interchangeably) was arriving. After he announced the good news, he told people to repent— to turn from their own ways—and believe in the good news of the new King. Yeshua taught that he himself was the new King, the promised Messiah of the Jewish people, who had come to pay the punishment everyone but the Messiah himself deserved. In probably the most well-known passage of the New Testament, Yeshua summarized his mission this way:

> "God so loved the world, that He gave His only Son, so

that everyone who believes in Him will not perish, but have eternal life. For God did not send the Son into the world to judge the world, but so that the world might be saved through Him." (John 3:16–17)

Yeshua's summary is consistent with the message that we saw in the Tanakh. God's plan from Psalm 2 was to overcome the world's evil by installing his son as the King. But first His son would be rejected, suffer, and die as a guilt offering for the people. And we know from Psalm 2 that anyone who gives their allegiance to the Son will live. We've seen enough evidence to be confident that Yeshua is the Messiah who fulfilled God's mission outlined in the Tanakh. And the way we get to experience the eternal life God provided us is by giving our allegiance to his Son.

One of Yeshua's closest students said it this way: "As many as received Him, to them He gave the right to become children of God, to those who believe in His name" (John 1:12)

God sent his Son Yeshua into the world because he wanted us to be his children. And if we receive Yeshua, if we trust in him, we will get to be children of God. This is the creator of the universe, our creator, telling us the purpose we were designed for: to "have life, and have it abundantly" (John 10:10). He's saying we can actually be exactly who we were intentionally designed and created to be by receiving and believing in Yeshua.

So, if we want to experience the eternal life God provided for us by sending his Son into the world to pay the price for our sin, we need to believe in his name. Another way of saying "believe in his name," in light of the whole biblical story, is to trust and follow Yeshua. But to trust him, we have to stop deciding what is good and evil for ourselves. Like Adam and Eve during their testing in the garden of Eden, we have a choice: determine what is good and bad for ourselves, which will bring evil into the world, whether we intend it or not; or trust God and follow what he says is good.

Yeshua and Gentiles

"I will say to those who were not My people,
'You are My people!'
And they will say, 'You are my God!'"

(Hosea 2:23)

If Yeshua's messianic mission was so Jewish, how come his gentile followers outnumber his Jewish followers? Is the God of Abraham, Isaac, and Jacob done with the Jewish people? Absolutely not. Yeshua went to the Jewish people first, but he did that to bless all nations.

Yeshua is the culmination of God's mission to crush the enemy and restore all of humanity back to relationship with himself. God announced at the beginning of the Torah that he had a plan to resolve the conflict humans created. The plan was to use the woman's offspring to crush the serpent while simultaneously being crushed himself. Starting with Abraham, the Jewish people were introduced as a piece of God's plan to resolve the conflict. God made a promise to Abraham that the seed would go through him. The rest of the biblical story is about God's developing plan to restore humanity to a relationship with himself and give the Jewish people a special place in that plan to restore all of mankind.

It's clear from the beginning of the Torah that God loves all people and is planning on rescuing all of them. We can even see it at the moment when God first called Abraham. When he gave the blessing to Abraham, he told him he was being blessed not only for his own benefit but so that all the nations of the world would experience blessing too.

"You shall be a blessing;
And I will bless those who bless you,
And the one who curses you I will curse.
And in you all the families of the earth will be blessed."

(Gen. 12:2–3)

God reminded the Jewish people of the way he planned to use them when they made the covenant at Mt. Sinai: "You shall be to Me a kingdom of priests and a holy nation.' These are the words that you [Moses] shall speak to the sons of Israel" (Ex. 19:6). We already looked at the various roles priests were responsible for, but their primary function involved intervening on behalf of the people. A kingdom of priests strongly implies they were to intercede on behalf of the nations. Especially in light of their heritage, descending from the man who God told He would use to bless all the nations.

The Prophets of the Tanakh told us time and time again that the gentiles would be included in God's rescue plan. Israel was supposed to be a kingdom of priests, that is, only if they kept all the laws they agreed to at Mt. Sinai (Ex.19:5-6). But they broke God's law, and God even told them they broke it (Ezek. 16:59).

So, Isaiah prophesied that the Messiah would rescue the whole world, including Jews and gentiles (Isa. 49:6). In this passage, Isaiah called the Messiah "Israel" because, as the proper King of Israel, if he did something, Israel did it. (Similarly, if Kim Jong Un signed an agreement with another nation, we might say North Korea signed a dealt with another nation.) Reading the whole passage, it is clear that Isaiah was specifically referring to the Messiah, the chief representative of Israel. Israel was supposed to be a light to the nations, but because the people of Israel broke the agreement, the Messiah, the priestly King of Israel, would be the light to the nations on behalf of Israel:

> He [God] says, "It is too small a thing that You should be My Servant
> To raise up the tribes of Jacob and to restore the protected ones of Israel;
> I will also make You a light of the nations
> So that My salvation may reach to the end of the earth."
>
> (Isa. 49:6)

In agreement that God's rescue plan did not end with the nation of Israel but extended to all the nations, the prophet Jeremiah added that

Israel and all of humanity would be gathered together. He associated the uniting of Jews and gentiles with the time when YHWH would make a new covenant with them:

> "Behold, days are coming," declares YHWH, "when I will sow the house of Israel and the house of Judah with the seed of mankind and the seed of animals. . . .
>
> "Behold, days are coming," declares YHWH, "when I will make a new covenant with the house of Israel and the house of Judah" (Jer. 31: 27, 31)

The New Testament author Paul, undoubtedly aware of Jeremiah, used a similar plant-based analogy when he wrote to the gentiles about their inclusion. Paul told the gentiles:

> Some of the branches were broken off, and you [Gentiles], being a wild olive, were grafted in among them [Israel] and became partaker with them of the rich root of the olive tree. (Rom. 11:17)

He told the gentiles that even though they had been far from the God of Israel, they would now be blessed from the same source as the Jewish people. The context of this passage is that Paul was reminding the gentiles that God cherishes the Jewish people. Although as a nation the Jewish people were currently rejecting their Messiah, Paul was explaining that God is not done with them.

> If you [Gentiles] were cut off from what is by nature a wild olive tree, and contrary to nature were grafted into a cultivated olive tree, how much more will these who are the natural branches be grafted into their own olive tree? (Rom. 11:24)

God planned to rescue both the Jewish people and the gentiles all along. He chose the Jewish people as his apparatus for restoring all peoples. Knowing that God intended to include all of creation in his rescue mission, it's easy to see why Yeshua's gentile followers outnumber his Jewish followers. There is only one Jewish people, but there have been thousands of gentile people groups. The gentiles of the world far outnumber the Jewish people of the world. So naturally there are more gentile people following Yeshua than Jewish people. This does not mean Yeshua has forgotten or is finished with the Jewish people. We'll see that he's not. Instead, it's good news that the light is spreading to the ends of the earth, beginning with Jerusalem: "I will also make You a light of the nation, so that My salvation may reach to the end of the earth."

Yeshua, the New Testament, and Being Jewish

Most people think that when a Jewish person begins to follow Yeshua, they are giving up their Jewish identity. This couldn't be further from the truth. You might be surprised to learn that the New Testament authors never once say or even imply that when a Jewish person begins to follow Yeshua, they need to give up their Jewishness. In fact, the New Testament authors teach the opposite, and they maintained their own Jewish identity while clearly following Yeshua.

Paul, the apostle, taught Yeshua's gentile followers that God is not done with the Jewish people. Paul obviously still considered himself Jewish. Paul asserted his Jewishness multiple times (e.g., Acts 21:39; 22:3). He even taught that not only is a person still Jewish when they follow Yeshua, but that the only way to truly live as a Jew was to follow the Jewish Messiah.

Sam Nadler, a Jewish follower of Yeshua, captures this idea beautifully:

> Yes, coming to faith in Messiah Yeshua is a radical change, a heart transformation of turning from sin and to God. That said, the New Covenant only builds upon and fulfills the ethical, moral and spiritual teaching and revelation of the God in the Hebrew Scriptures. So, in the New Covenant we read that the early believers continued attending the Temple and synagogue, kept the feasts, circumcised their

Jewish children, and kept other aspects of the Law. This was not to deny Messiah's authority or to show they merited righteousness, but for the sake of identifying with their own people and honoring the Lord. In short, they remained Jewish.[14]

Nadler was expressing that, for a Jewish person as well as for a gentile, following Yeshua is a radical change. It means letting go of our desires and trusting that God's way is purer and will benefit us more. But while what Yeshua asks of us is life changing, what Yeshua does not ask us to do is abandon our Jewishness.

The reason this concept is foreign to many Jewish people, and even many Christians, probably has a lot to do with church history. It's no secret that people have oppressed and persecuted the Jewish people, claiming to do so in the name of Yeshua throughout history.

But anyone acting in hatred towards the Jewish people would be guilty of using the Lord's name in vain, thereby breaking the Ten Commandments. These anti-Semitic people pursued their own agenda, unleashing their own hate and stamping Yeshua's name on it to validate their cause. If someone has received Yeshua and read his words, they should clearly see that he is the king of the Jews who weeps for Jerusalem (Luke 19:41). The life and teachings of Yeshua are all about love and leave no room for hatred of anyone. The hatred of the Jewish people is anti-Yeshua. Antisemitism is not only anti-Jewish but also goes against everything Yeshua stood for.

One of Yeshua's closest students, John the apostle, explained that the person who knows God will be loving, and if someone is not exhibiting love, they don't truly know Yeshua. Have you ever known someone so happy and kind that being around them makes you happier and kinder as well? I definitely do. John explained that knowing God has the same effect. If you know God, you won't be hateful. You'll be loving.

> Beloved, let's love one another; for love is from God, and whoever loves has been born of God and knows God. The one who does not love does not know God, because God

is love. (1 John 4:7–8)

In the New Covenant, God is not done with the Jewish people. He hasn't rejected them. He loves them (Rom. 11:28). Yeshua loves the Jewish people. His whole gospel mission begins with the Jewish people and extends to the gentiles (Rom. 1:16). Yeshua does not call us to abandon our Jewish identity; rather, he is the fulfillment of our Jewish identity. He is the promised King of the Jews who was always going to bring God's deliverance to the world. Again, if Yeshua really is the Jewish Messiah—and we have enough evidence to be sure that he is—then the least Jewish thing we can do is reject him. The Jewish way must be to receive him, put our trust in him, and follow him. In Yeshua's own words, "I am the way, and the truth, and the life; no one comes to the Father except through me" (John 14:6).

Chapter 5: Summary

Part 1: The New Testament sees itself as the fulfillment of the Tanakh

1. Yeshua taught that the whole Tanakh was about himself (Luke 14:44; John 5:46)
2. The New Testament authors clearly believed Yeshua's life and teachings were rooted in the Tanakh (Matt. 1; Mark 1:1–3; John 1:1–5; Tim. 3:15).

Part 2: Most of the evidence for Yeshua's life, death, and resurrection come from the writings of the New Testament. There are numerous other sources, but they mainly serve to corroborate the information in the New Testament instead of adding new information.

1. The writings of the New Testament are trustworthy because:
    a. We have a solid chain of possession linking the authors to their books.
    b. The authors were eyewitnesses or overseen by eyewitnesses.
    c. The authors intended their stories to be believed.
    d. There is definitive evidence from inside the Christian community, from outside the community, and from enemies of Christians that the earliest Christians were actively hunted down and persecuted for claiming to have seen Yeshua after he rose from the dead.
        i. At least nine of the NT authors suffered and died for what they claimed to have seen without redacting any statements. They were doing their best to record Yeshua's life accurately

Part 3: Yeshua fits all the descriptions outlined for the Messiah in the Tanakh

1. Yeshua is the Son of God and also one with God.
    a. In Matthew 3:17, God announces that Yeshua is his Son (cf.

Ps. 2:6; Isa. 53:5; Zech. 12:10).

2. Yeshua was fully righteous and without sin.
   a. The New Testament authors view Yeshua as being totally sinless (1 John 3:5; Heb. 4:15).
   b. The narrative in the New Testament shows Yeshua passing the same test that Adam and Eve failed in another "garden moment." Yeshua labeled his moment of desire and, unlike the first couple, trusted God instead (Luke 42:44; Matt. 4:3–11).

3. Yeshua was rejected by his generation. He suffered and died by crucifixion.
   a. There are four independent detailed eyewitness accounts of Yeshua's trials and crucifixion recorded in the New Testament.
   b. The Roman historian and enemy of Christianity, Tacitus, corroborated Yeshua's crucifixion, adding that it was the most extreme form of punishment.

4. Yeshua rose from the dead.
   a. Independent accounts of Yeshua's death record that large crowds knew about Yeshua being in the city during the week of his crucifixion (Matt. 21:1–10; John 12: 12–13; Mark 11:1–11; Luke 19: 29–40); the Talmud admits that Yeshua performed miracles; and both Tacitus and Josephus record that Yeshua amassed a large following.
   b. Yeshua's trials were public, and since Jerusalem is small in size, everyone would have known that Yeshua was crucified.
   c. Yeshua was buried in a member of the Sanhedrin's tomb. This was public knowledge and couldn't have been a lie, because it would have been immediately falsifiable in Jerusalem.
   d. Jerusalem, the only city where Christianity was immediately verifiable or falsifiable, is where Christianity

first exploded (Acts 2:41-47). This is corroborated by Tacitus, Annals 15.44.

Part 4: Yeshua's messianic mission was the good news that the kingdom of heaven was arriving on earth through King Yeshua, who had come to get rid of evil. Just as it was written in the Tanakh, the way he did so was to take the punishment of sin on himself so we could have life with God forever. Yeshua taught that if we turn from our sin and trust him, we'll experience that life.

Part 5: Jewish people and gentiles in the New Testament:

1. Yeshua's rescue plan came to the Jewish people first, but his saving work extends to all people, just like the Tanakh said it would. Naturally, most of Yeshua's followers would be gentiles, because most people are gentiles.

2. Even though God's rescue plan extends to the gentiles and many people have been actively antisemitic in the name of Yeshua, antisemitism is not tolerated in the life and teachings of Yeshua nor anywhere in the New Testament. People who act antisemitically in the name of Yeshua are wrongly using his name to justify their own agendas.

6

Common Concerns

The Oneness of God and the Father, Son, and Holy Spirit

A common misconception about the New Testament is that it teaches belief in three gods. I mean, look, the Trinity is a core idea in Christianity. Everyone knows the Trinity is three Gods—case closed, right? Well . . . no.

The word *trinity* is a contraction of *tri-unity*. So, the label "Trinity" is intended to emphasize God's oneness. God is one. But we need to look at what the Torah teaches about the oneness of God.

Before the time of Yeshua, many early Jewish scholars read Scripture and knew that God somehow was at the same time "one" but also not quite solitary. Respected Jewish interpretations of the Tanakh in the Second Temple period attempted to make sense of this.

In two essential Jewish works that predated Yeshua, 1 Enoch and 4 Ezra, the authors clearly believed there was a divine human figure ruling alongside God (1 Enoch 48: 2–6; cf. 62:6–7). The scroll of 4 Ezra mentions that the human-like being who ruled alongside God also existed before creation with the Most High. The understanding of some sort of multiplicity within God's oneness was not a new understanding of Scripture.

Okay, so it isn't a new idea, but is it the correct interpretation of Scripture? We have a central and very significant verse to interpret. The Shema has been on the lips of the Jewish people for thousands of years, and for good reason. It is a really important verse. We absolutely should not just ignore the Shema. The New Covenant is firmly rooted in the Tanakh, so if the New and Old Covenants disagree on who God is, then the New Covenant can't be correct. Let's examine the Shema, the Tanakh as a whole, and what the New Covenant teaches to see if we can discern who God tells us he is.

> "Hear, Israel! YHWH is our God, YHWH is one [*echad*]! And you shall love YHWH your God with all your heart and with all your soul and with all your strength. These words, which I am commanding you today, shall be on your heart." (Deut.6:4–6)

The Hebrew word for "one," *echad*, is a unique word. Before we do anything else, let's just look at one of the first appearances of *echad* in the Torah.

> For this reason a man shall leave his father and his mother, and be joined to his wife; and they shall become one [*echad*] flesh (Gen. 2:24).

Here the Torah uses the word *echad* to show "oneness," it's speaking of two people being united together as one entity. It's talking about a unity. And "unity" is a great way to describe what *echad* means. You might think, "Okay, but that's just the Hebrew word for 'one,' right? The authors had to use the words at their disposal, and the word for 'one' and 'unity' just happens to be the same."

Actually no. The Torah authors had another word for "one" that they could have used to show the only-ness of God if that's what they had wanted to do. There is another Hebrew word that the biblical authors use several times, but never to describe God. The word *yached* means "one" but carries a different connotation than *echad*. While *echad* means a multiplicity in one, or unity, *yached* means one and only. So, the word "one" in the Shema does not teach us that God is an isolated God and cannot be a unity; instead, it even implies that he is some sort of multiplicity in one.

Elohim

We are introduced to God on the first page, in the first sentence of the Bible: "In the beginning God [Elohim] created the heavens and the earth" (Gen. 1:1). It's curious that the word first used for God, and used over two thousand times in the Bible, has a plural ending. In Hebrew, to make a masculine word plural, you add on *im*, very similar to adding an *s* in English.

The Torah also gives us a glimpse into how God refers to himself: "Then God said, 'Let Us make mankind in Our image, according to Our likeness" (Gen. 1:26). Notice that God uses the plural words *us* and *our* to refer to himself.

Some say that maybe this kind of language is used to show the royalty or nobility of God. In ancient Greece, Alexander the Great referred to himself as "us" in a show of "plurality of majesty." In the ancient Greek world, this was a standard practice. But the writing of the Torah is thousands of years earlier than the introduction of this norm. So, although thousands of years later, Greeks used "us" to talk about "me," this was not a usage of the word in ancient Hebrew. Not one of the Hebrew kings is ever referred to in the "plurality of majesty."

Others say God was talking to the angels: "Hey, angels, let us make man in our image." This theory is even less credible. The very next sentence shows that man was created in the image of God and God alone; humans were not created in the image of angels. "God created man in His own image, in the image of God He created him; male and female He created them" (Gen. 1:27). That means God sees himself as an "us," and he can refer to his image as "our" image.

This nature of God existing as some sort of multiplicity in one—unity—is why we come across interesting passages of Scripture. For instance, YHWH appeared to Abraham along with two angels and ate with him. Then YHWH told Abraham he was going to destroy Sodom. So YHWH was on earth at this point, and Scripture tells us, "Then YHWH rained brimstone and fire on Sodom and Gomorrah from YHWH out of heaven" (Gen. 19:24).

YHWH was on earth, but he rained brimstone and fire from YHWH out of heaven. The Torah is depicting YHWH as two distinct people in two places at once. This depiction of God existing as a multiplicity in one appears all over Scripture, notably the first time God reveals his name YHWH.

In Exodus 3, there is an intentional and glaringly obvious confusion about who is appearing to Moses in the burning bush. The authors tell us that the angel of YHWH appeared to Moses from within the bush (Ex. 3:2). Then the authors tell us that YHWH, God himself, is the one who spoke to Moses from within the bush (Ex.3:6,7,14). The angel of YHWH who appeared to Moses says "EHYH ASER EHYH," which means "*I* am He that exists." This name is so distinct to God, that when God told Moses how to repeat his name to Israel, Moses had to say a different version of the same name: "YHWH," which means "*He* is He that exists." Nobody except God himself can correctly say EHYH ASER EHYH. Yet the angel of YHWH says the version that God alone can say. So, the angel of YHWH is portrayed as distinct from YHWH but also as YHWH himself. Mind-boggling, yes, but also clear.

God the Father

Does the Tanakh teach us anything else about the nature of this God? Yes, the Tanakh teaches that God is Father, Son, and Spirit and that God is one. When Yeshua came, he revealed this more clearly, and it became more understandable, but it was not absent from the Tanakh. We can see the Father, Son, and Spirit in the one God by reading the Tanakh.

God is Father. That is essential to who he is: "I am a Father to Israel" (Jer. 31:9; cf. Deut. 1:21; 8:5; Ex. 4:22; Isa 1:2).

> "How I would set you among My sons
> And give you a pleasant land,
> The most beautiful inheritance of the nations!'
> And I said, 'You shall call Me, My Father,
> And not turn away from following Me."
>
> (Jer. 3:19)

Everything God does stems from his fatherhood. He creates and rules his creation as Father. As Michael Reeves puts it, "If, before all things, God was eternally a Father, then this God is an inherently outgoing life-giving God. He did not give life for the first time when he decided to create; from eternity he has been life-giving."[1]

A father can't be a father without a child. But we know God is not dependent on his creation to make him who he is. He is not a lonely, needy God who needed to be a father but had no children. God is Father because he has been eternally giving life to the his Son (Ps. 2:7; Isa. 42:1). This means the Son is eternal as well. The pre-Christian Jewish interpreters knew that God has eternally been a father. That's why they wrote about the divine-human Son of God (1 Enoch 48:2–6, together with 62:6–7 and 4 Ezra). Yeshua and the New Testament authors were not adding anything new when they described God as an eternal Father. They were revealing more about the relationship between the Father and the Son. They taught that the Father has eternally loved the Son, and the Father's love prompts the Son to love the Father in return.

> "The Father loves the Son and has entrusted all things to His hand." (John 3:35)

> "So that the world may know that I love the Father, I do exactly as the Father commanded Me." (John 14:31)

God the Spirit

Time and time again we see the Spirit of God acting on God's behalf, somehow a distinct person, yet one with God. The prophet Isaiah understood God's Spirit in this way: "Now YHWH God has sent Me, and His Spirit" (Isa. 48:16). If we go back to the first page of the Bible again, we encounter the Spirit of God: "The earth was a formless and desolate emptiness, and darkness was over the surface of the deep, and the Spirit [*ruakh*] of God was hovering over the surface of the waters" (Gen. 1:2).

Ruakh is the Hebrew word for breath, wind, and spirit. In the minds of the biblical authors, these things are deeply connected. They don't have distinct meanings like homonyms. The Torah speaks of our breath being God's own ruakh that we have borrowed (Gen. 6:3).

Even the wind is seen as deeply connected to this idea of God's Spirit in creation. After flooding the earth, God causes the flood to subside by sending a "ruakh" over the waters, similar to how his ruakh hovered over the waters in Genesis 1:2. So, God can send his Spirit to go act on his behalf; his Spirit is one with him, yet somehow distinct. This explains why the prophet Isa. said that God sent him and his Spirit.

The New Testament authors tell us that the way the Father loves his Son is by giving him his Spirit. Paul told us that God loves his people in the same way, by giving us his Spirit (Rom. 5:5). After Yeshua was baptized by John (the prophet of Malachi 4:5 who, in the Spirit of Elijah, heralded the coming of the Messiah), God's Spirit hovered on Yeshua over the waters.

> Immediately coming up out of the water, He [Yeshua] saw the heavens opening, and the Spirit, like a dove, descending upon Him; and a voice came from the heavens: "You are My beloved Son; in You I am well pleased." (Mark 1:10–11)

Relationship is intrinsic to God. He has been in real relationship for all of eternity. He did not need to create in order to be Father, Son, or Spirit; he has always been all three. God is inherently Father, Son, and Spirit in loving relationship, and he decided to share that relationship with us. So he created us, and we get to benefit from his life-giving Fatherly love. Sam Nadler expressed this excellently: "Since relationship is intrinsic to the triune God, it is intrinsic to our lives as well."[2]

Didn't Yeshua Take Away from the Law?

> "Whatever I command you, you shall be careful to do; you shall not add to nor take anything away from it." (Deut. 12:32)

During the life of the sinai covenant, God told Israel that because they had broken their covenant, in the messianic age he would make a new covenant with Israel and the gentiles. (Jer. 31:27–34) As the Messiah, Yeshua inaugurated this new covenant. That does not mean Yeshua abolished or did away with the Torah. In fact, speaking of what the Tanakh instructed, Yeshua said, "Do not presume that I came to abolish the Law or the Prophets; I did not come to abolish, but to fulfill" (Matt. 5:17). So, we have to look at what the function and purpose of the laws were to see if Yeshua fulfilled them or was just making an excuse.

In the Torah, the laws given to Israel can be understood in three categories. There were civil laws for the theocracy of Israel to govern its people. These laws applied to the government of Israel, governed under the Torah.

The next category of law was the ceremonial laws. These laws in the Torah give instructions on gaining right standing before God, such as keeping kosher, sacrifices, and ceremonies regarding cleanness (Lev. 19:2; 20:7–8; Ex. 19:5; 1 Peter 1:2). Ceremonial laws could also be the rituals that helped Israel remember what God had done for them so they would recognize how he would work in the future; examples would be Shabbat and the annual feasts. Ceremonial laws could also be specific regulations, such as kosher laws and clothing restrictions, that distinguished Israel from its pagan neighbors.

Finally, the Torah contains moral laws. The moral laws are an overflow of God's good character. God is good, so he instructs his people to be good. The moral laws show us what is holy, just, and good. They are the laws that teach us how to love God with all our heart, soul, and might and how to love others as ourselves. These could be laws regarding sexual conduct, treating others with respect, and other ethical commandments.

When Yeshua said he came to fulfill the Torah and the Prophets, he was saying that the purpose of everything written in the Torah and the Prophets was to point to him. The purpose of the Law, then, was so that the Jewish people would recognize the rescue plan when he arrived. Take Passover for an example: The Jewish people were instructed in the covenant to keep Passover every year. In the Torah there's no seder; there are instructions on how to keep Passover, but there is actually a lot of freedom in how the people can keep the feast. God told them why they were supposed to keep it every year: so that they would always remember how he saved them from their slavery in Egypt (Ex.12:27). Keeping the Passover every year is similar to how schools regularly practice fire drills. When the real fire happens, the students should know what to do.

On the first Passover night, God had them slaughter a lamb and smear its blood on the door. When the angel of death saw the blood on the door, the angel would pass over, and the firstborn in that house wouldn't die (Ex. 12:21–23). It should have been no surprise, then, that Yeshua was called the Passover lamb and then was sacrificed on Passover (John 1:36; 1 Cor. 5:7; Matt. 26:1–2; Sanhedrin 43: a20). When Yeshua said he was the fulfillment of the Law and the Prophets, he was referring to this type of fulfillment. Everything that was commanded in the Torah came to its culmination in him. The first Passover's lamb sacrifice delivered the people from death and their slavery in Egypt, but Yeshua's work as the ultimate Passover Lamb delivers us from our enslavement to sin. That is a much bigger deal leading to a far greater outcome (1 Cor. 5:1–7).

Sacrifices in general, not just the Passover sacrifice, were key ceremonial laws that pointed to Yeshua. The Torah taught that it is blood that makes atonement for sins: "The life of the flesh is in the blood, and I have given it to you on the altar to make atonement for your souls; for it is the blood by reason of the life that makes atonement" (Lev. 17:11). If it is blood that makes atonement for sins, then we need a sacrifice for our sins if we are to avoid the penalty of sin—for "the soul who sins will die" (Ezek. 18:4). This sacrifice needed to be the Messiah:

> He was pierced for our offenses,
> He was crushed for our wrongdoings;
> The punishment for our well-being was laid upon Him,
> And by His wounds we are healed.
>
> (Isa. 53:5).

The New Testament authors said that the laws in the old covenant were shadows of the things to come, and the thing casting the shadow was Yeshua. The old covenant was something like a syllabus: Everything in the first semester serves to prepare for the final exam, but it isn't the final exam. The Messiah is. The laws of the old covenant were given so we would recognize and follow the Messiah, Yeshua, upon his arrival. Yeshua inaugurated the new covenant through his death on the cross, and now those who receive him are no longer under the first covenant.

That said, the ceremonial laws performed an important function: They symbolized the people's holiness before God. Holiness means being set apart, or unique, for God. So, if Yeshua fulfilled the Law, do we still need to keep all the ceremonial laws such as keeping kosher and sacrificing in the temple? No, we don't have to. Yeshua's sacrifice covers all our sins. We can keep those laws if we are keeping them to remember what Yeshua did—but we don't *have* to keep them if we give our allegiance to Yeshua. That's because he will send God's Spirit to dwell in us.

It's the Spirit of God that sets us apart in the new covenant. Under the old covenant, the Spirit of God was dangerous. People couldn't approach the presence of God because they were unclean. (Lev. 16:2) But once they are covered by the blood of the righteous Passover Lamb, Yeshua, the Holy Spirit indwells God's children and sets them apart.

The *civil laws* were laws for the general governing of the nation.

These naturally applied only to the theocracy of Israel, and once Israel was no longer governing itself under the Torah, those laws could no longer be properly practiced. The *ceremonial laws* all pointed to Yeshua, and he fulfilled them. But the *moral laws* are an overflow of God's good, loving character, so Yeshua and the New Testament authors teach us that, as children of God, we should be good as God is good. It is therefore good to follow the moral laws of the old covenant, which teach us what good looks like. Since we are now under King Yeshua's new covenant, we are free from the Law. But the New Testament authors teach us that this freedom does not mean we aren't sinning if we break the moral laws. It just means this sin no longer leads to death if you are sealed in the new covenant by the Holy Spirit—because the new covenant is a covenant of grace (Rom. 6:14–16).

Virgins Can't Give Birth

The virgin birth is impossible as far as science goes. It's just not how the human body works; the egg needs to be fertilized.

But then, wooden staffs can't turn into living snakes, looking at a serpent lifted up on a pole can't heal you from deadly snake venom, the sun can't be delayed from setting, and a sea can't split in half on command to reveal dry ground. Yet each of these impossibilities, and many more, are miracles recorded in the Tanakh. Saying God can't make a virgin give birth is equivalent to saying God can't act outside any of the laws of nature. If God can't make a virgin give birth, then he is governed by the same laws of nature that he created.

If God is powerful enough to create the universe and everything in it, wouldn't he be able to control and manipulate that universe easily? If God designed the human body and brought it into existence from nothing, then it would be no challenge at all for him to enter what he created and supernaturally intervene. Yes, this would break the laws of science. But nobody is claiming that God is restrained by the laws of science. Science is necessarily the study of the natural world; God is outside of the natural world, and the natural world is controlled by him. So, could a God who created the natural world, and who is not constrained by its laws as we are, enter into that world and temporarily pause those rules? Of course he could.

This idea can be compared to the movie *The Matrix*. Everyone in the Matrix is governed by the laws of the Matrix universe. But there are people who exist outside the Matrix, and when they enter into the Matrix, they are not confined by its laws.

A person who says God can't perform miracles doesn't really believe in God. If there really is an extremely powerful, uncaused eternal being who created the universe, then this being would have no difficulty entering into his creation and acting outside the rules that he set in place to sustain it.

To say God cannot exist because miracles are impossible is assuming the conclusion and then arguing from it. It's assuming your argument is right and saying, essentially, "My position is right because my position is the only correct way." This logical fallacy is called *begging the question*. An obvious example of begging the question would be: "Smoking causes cancer because the smoke from cigarettes is a carcinogen." I tried to prove that smoking causes cancer by saying smoking is cancerous; I've reworded the conclusion and called it a reason. Similarly, saying God doesn't exist because miracles are impossible is starting at the end and calling the position a reason.

If the God of the Torah exists, then not only is a miraculous birth possible, it's actually likely. After all, Yeshua's miraculous birth is not the first miraculous birth in the biblical story; several in the lineage of the promised Messiah experienced some sort of miracle birth. God promised the Messiah would come through Abraham and Sarah, but the couple lived long lives without any children because Sarah was barren. Then when Abraham was ninety-nine, God appeared to him and told him he would have a child the following year. Sarah realized this was humanly impossible, so she laughed. God responded, "Is anything too difficult for YHWH? At the appointed time I will return to you, at this time next year, and Sarah will have a son" (Gen. 18:14). The birth of Isaac, through whom the Messiah would come, was miraculous.

Isaac, who was born miraculously, married Rebekah. Rebekah

was also barren, so Isaac prayed to God to give them a child. Again God intervened and caused Rebekah to miraculously bear a child (Gen. 25:21). Rebekah had twins, Jacob, and Esau. God revealed to Rebekah that Jacob would be the one through whom the promised blessing, the Messiah, would come.

Jacob had two wives, the sisters Rachel and Leah. Jacob loved Rachel, but like Rebekah and Sarah before her, she was barren (Gen. 29:31). (The Torah tells us that the only reason Leah wasn't barren is because God allowed her to have children, meaning God was in control of her childbearing as well, even if it might not seem as miraculous.) But again God stepped in miraculously and provided Rachel a miracle birth (Gen. 30:22–23).

So, if you think that a virgin birth is impossible, but you believe in the God of the Tanakh, he would ask you, as he asked Abraham long ago, "Is anything too difficult for YHWH?" In following the story of the Jewish people, we see a pattern of miracle births, so we should expect the Messiah to be born miraculously.

Why does God work through these miracle births? Again, it's about trusting him. God made a promise to Abraham and Sarah that He would provide them with an heir. Abraham believed God and his belief was counted to him as righteousness (Gen. 15:6). But after some time, Abraham and Sarah's trust wavered, and they decided they should help God produce the promised blessing instead of relying on God to do it his way. Sarah convinced Abraham to sleep with her Egyptian slave so they would get an offspring that way (Gen. 16: 1-6). Abraham did have a son with the slave and named him Ishmael. God blessed the son, but he told Abraham that Ishmael would not be the son through whom the promised blessing would come. The Messiah wouldn't come through Ishmael.

This time it was Abraham who laughed out of unbelief, just as Sarah had done. He said, "God, I already have a son. Just use him. Sarah can't have children." But God reemphasized his promise and said, "No, I'll do it through Sarah" (Gen. 17:15–19). It's important to God that we know he can deliver on his promises. When we know God is powerful enough to deliver, we can rest confident he will provide.

From the narrative pattern alone we should expect a miraculous birth for the Messiah. But the virgin birth of the Messiah was also specifically prophesied in the Tanakh. In Genesis 3:15, when God first announced his messianic plan, we get the first little clue:

> "I will make enemies
> Of you and the woman,
> And of your offspring and her Descendant;
> He shall bruise you on the head,
> And you shall bruise Him on the heel."

From the very beginning God promised to defeat the serpent, Satan, who introduced evil to humanity by using the offspring of the woman. It's interesting that God specifically said he would use the descendant of the woman instead of the descendent of Adam, who was ultimately responsible for their sin. Eve had consequences too, but at the very least, this detail is interesting, and we should pay attention to it.

Later, the prophet Isaiah shed more light on this: "Therefore YHWH Himself will give you a sign: Behold, the virgin will conceive and give birth to a son, and she will name Him Immanuel" (Isa. 7:14).

Typically, rabbis object to this translation. They say that "virgin" is an inaccurate translation of the Hebrew word *almah*; that word just refers to a young maiden, they say. But the Tanakh only used the Hebrew word six other times, and in every instance, *almah* is clearly used for a young girl who has not yet had sex (Gen. 24:43; Ex. 2:8; Prov. 30:18; Ps. 68:25; Song 1:3; 6:8). If Isaiah did not mean a virgin, he wouldn't have used the word *almah*.

The leading Jewish scholarship of the first and second centuries BCE understood that Isaiah 7:14 was speaking of an actual virgin. These men who translated the Tanakh into Greek for the Septuagint hundreds of years before Yeshua's birth translated *almah* to the Greek *parthenos*. And there is no dispute over the word *parthenos*; it means "virgin." This tells us that before Yeshua's virgin birth, Jewish scholars knew the Messiah would be born from a virgin, because they read Scripture. The first-ever Jewish translation of Hebrew Scripture translated *almah* as "virgin." Not until after Yeshua did rabbis question the translation, attempting to invalidate Yeshua's claim to the throne by manipulating Scripture.

How Could Yeshua Be the Son of David?

Several prophecies in the Tanakh make it clear that the Messiah will come through the line of David. There's no doubt about it: He's referred to as a son of David, as the righteous branch of David, as the root of Jesse (David's Dad), and the like. This Davidic descendance is a key eligibility requirement for the Messiah (Isa. 9:7; 11:1; Jer. 23:5-6).

Most people find genealogies boring or confusing, but in this case, it's important that we examine the confusion. Some say that if the New Testament is to be believed, then Yeshua can't be from the line of David because he has no earthly father; his mother was a virgin when he was conceived. Others, later rabbis like Maimonides have taught that Yeshua was not from the line of David and that his father was actually a gentile. Still others, say the lineage of Yeshua recorded in the New Testament contradicts itself or disqualifies him. We'll briefly examine each of these thoughts and, hopefully, bring a smidge of life to normally dry genealogy.

Let's look at the first claim: The New Testament made a fool of itself because Yeshua couldn't be a descendant of King David and at the same time have no earthly father. Yet the New Testament would have us believe both are true—really? The answer is yes. The entire Bible, not just the New Testament, teaches that those two claims are not at odds with each other. Yeshua was considered the legal son of Joseph, a descendant of David. Luke records this for us in the official language of the time: "As was commonly held" (Luke 3:23) was the Greek term for something being legally confirmed. In the Hebrew Bible, legal guardianship is considered authentic fatherhood. We have examples of this legal guardianship not only being endorsed by God in the Torah, but in a way that is important to the origins of the Jewish people.

Don't believe me? Name all the tribes of Israel. If you were actually able to name all thirteen tribes, congratulations. That's right: There are *thirteen* tribes of Israel. Two of them are half-tribes, because the patriarch Joseph's sons were legally adopted by Jacob. God approved and endorsed this legal status by making them tribes of Israel (Gen. 48:4–6). Maybe because of this story, maybe for another reason, early Jewish culture has always considered the legal father to be the father in every respect.[3]

So, the absence of a biological earthly father doesn't diminish Yeshua's claim to the throne in any capacity. There is already a biblical precedent for God's operating through legal guardianship. And this is without even mentioning that Yeshua's biological mother was also descended from King David. (Luke 3:23–38)

On to the second concern. Some later Rabbis have taught that Yeshua wasn't descended from David. There are major problems with these rabbis' claims. Yeshua was a public figure, and it was hotly debated during his time whether or not he was the Messiah. At his trial, the high priest asked him if he was the Messiah (Mark 14: 61). During Yeshua's time many people, especially the Pharisees and priests, accused Yeshua of not being the Messiah for a multitude of reasons. But nobody ever claimed he wasn't descended from David. Since being a son of David was an essential qualification, somebody would have raised that objection if he wasn't.

The genealogical scrolls were easily accessible and stored in the temple, so the very priests who accused Yeshua had access to his lineage. But those who tried to prove he wasn't the Messiah never claimed he wasn't descended from David.

Unfortunately, the genealogical scrolls were later lost to history when the temple was destroyed.[4] But the claim that Yeshua wasn't descended from King David was never raised when those scrolls were accessible. Not until hundreds and hundreds of years after the scrolls were destroyed did that argument appear. By then it was impossible to prove that *anyone* was descended from the line of David, and this remains the case today. In Yeshua's day, though, the scrolls were readily available and Yeshua's lineage easily provable. Had he not been a son of David, all his enemies would have pounced on the opportunity to discredit him.

Now to the last concern: that the New Testament genealogies either contradict each other or disqualify Yeshua from messiahship. The New Testament does record two different genealogies of Yeshua. The differences aren't in two or three names way in the middle somewhere; rather, two entirely different genealogies are traced from David. They contain two names in common, but those names refer to different people and the similarities are coincidental. After David, the genealogies only have one actual person in common, and that is Yeshua's legal guardian, Joseph. It is highly unlikely that the gospel writers Matthew and Luke, two of Yeshua's closest followers who meticulously recorded Yeshua's life, would get something this important so wrong.

The reason is simple. The genealogies are different because Matthew was tracing Yeshua's lineage through his legal guardian, Joseph, who was descended from King David (Matt. 1:1–12). And Luke was tracing Yeshua's lineage through Mary, also descended from King David but through another of David's sons. Luke traced the line through Mary and then attached it to Joseph (Luke 3:23–37).

How and why did he attach Mary's lineage to Joseph? First, there was no term for son-in-law at that time. Also, we know that legal fatherhood was considered fully valid. So, when Joseph married Mary, he was really, authentically considered the son of Mary's father. Luke attached Joseph to the lineage instead of Mary because in the first century the mother's lineage wasn't valid. There really would be no other reasonable alternatives for why the two genealogies are entirely different. If Matthew and Luke were both recording the genealogy of Yeshua from the same parent, surely these two gospel writers who were so close with Yeshua and his mother would have known the name of Yeshua's grandfather. If it was an issue with accuracy, there would be at least some people in common, at least his grandfather.

The other reservation some have with the New Testament genealogy is that on Joseph's side, Matthew records that Yeshua comes through the line of Jeconiah. Jeconiah was a descendent of King David whom God cursed:

This is what YHWH says:

> "Record this man down as childless,
> A man who will not prosper in his days;
> For no man among his descendants will prosper
> Sitting on the throne of David
> Or ruling again in Judah."
>
> (Jer. 2:30)

Jeconiah was indeed cursed that none of his descendants would sit on David's throne. But God is "a gracious and compassionate God, slow to anger and abundant in mercy, and One who relents of disaster" (Jonah 4:2), a God who doesn't make the child suffer for the sins of the father (Ezek. 18:20; Jer. 31:30). So, God undid this curse and blessed Zerubbabel, Jeconiah's grandson, to be king over Israel on David's throne (Hag. 2:23).

This is hard to understand in our culture. When most of us hear the word *cursed*, we think of Harry Potter. It's as if, when God curses someone, he's casting a spell on them that will permanently cripple them. But that's not the way the Bible uses the language of cursing and blessing. In the Tanakh, curses are the natural result of sin, the evil consequences that come from rebelling against God. But the God of Israel delights in undoing curses that people bring on themselves. He is forgiving and wants to bless them. God's mission, from the first pages of the Bible, has been to undo the curse that mankind brought on creation and restore us to blessing. So, God undid the curse Jeconiah brought on his descendants and instead blessed his descendant Zerubbabel and, later, Yeshua.

Why Isn't There Peace?

> "There will be no end to the increase of His government
> or of peace
> On the throne of David and over his kingdom,
> To establish it and to uphold it with justice and

righteousness
From then on and forevermore.
The zeal of YHWH of armies will accomplish this."
(Isa. 9:7)

We know the Messiah is supposed to establish peace, so if Yeshua is the Messiah, how come we don't see peace on earth now?

The messianic promise of peace is about so much more than just a worldly peace. The word *shalom* in the messianic prophecies for peace refers to the webbing together of all that a human is. It refers to one's personal peace, relational peace, peace with nature, and peace with God. It recalls the peace we had in the garden of Eden when we dwelt with God, before Adam and Eve tried to take control. After that, all these things spiraled into chaos. First and foremost, the relationship between God and people was tarnished and God separated humans from himself (Gen. 3:24).

Peace with nature was also interrupted. In the garden, God provided nourishment for people in abundance, and it didn't require life-draining work. But after humans tried to take control, from God, life-draining work is exactly what happened; because of their sin, the work people had to do to sustain their lives became inherently draining. God told Adam, "By the sweat of your face you shall eat bread, until you return to the ground." (Gen. 3:19).

People's relational peace was also shattered by Adam and Eve's rebellion. Men and women were equal in God's eyes, and they were supposed to be joined together as one flesh. But now that they had brought evil into the world, God told them that even this relational peace would dwindle: "Your desire will be for your husband," he told Eve, "and he shall rule over you" (v. 16). God had created men and women to be equal, but now the peace that they had toppled, and the man started to rule over his wife instead of co-ruling with her as God intended (Gen. 1:28).

When the Messiah came to bring peace, he came to restore this true peace we had in the garden. The personal, and relational peace was a natural overflow of Adam and Eve's good relationship with God

(Isa. 26:3). That's a peace that by necessity must start with God's dealing with sin and restoring people to himself. It brings us back to Yeshua's messianic mission: to rid evil from the world, starting with our thoughts.

So, why don't we have peace on earth? Because God is still allowing people who reject him to live in his creation. For those who have accepted him, he has begun the work of making them holy, and he will bring it to completion when he totally removes sin from the world. One day that time will come. God will permanently separate all those people who won't let him transform them. And creation will be restored to the way it was in the garden.

Messiah is called the "Prince of Peace" (Isa. 9:6) And when he returns to reign there will be peace on earth (Isa. 2:1–4; 9:7). But in order for there to be earthly peace, he must first deal with the conflict between us and him and restore us to the proper relationship with him that we were created for. In his mercy for the people he loves, his judgment day drags on so that humans have more opportunity to receive his rescue. But he won't let his creation be plagued with evil forever. One day he is going to separate those who refuse his peace (Mal. 4:1–3; Ps. 1:4–6; Heb. 10:37).

When we follow Yeshua, we will continue to live in the world that presently has conflict and "tribulation." But the peace Yeshua brought starts with our relationship with him, and it overflows into our lives. So even though we live in a world full of trouble, we have peace.

Yeshua said, "These things I have spoken to you so that in Me you may have peace. In the world you have tribulation, but take courage; I have overcome the world" (John 16:33). Right now we have peace in Yeshua, even as we live in a tumultuous world. But soon Yeshua will return and reign, and on that day his kingdom will be one of complete and lasting peace (Isa. 9:7).

Chapter 6: Summary

Part 1: The Oneness of God and the Father, Son, and Holy Spirit

1. The New Testament does not teach three gods. In fact the word *tri-unity* is intended to emphasize the oneness of God.

2. The oneness of God was biblically defined using the word *echad*, which means multiplicity in unity. There is another Hebrew word for "one" in the biblical vocabulary that means a solitary one. The Tanakh authors intentionally chose *echad* instead.

3. God refers to himself with plural possessive pronouns: "Then God said, let Us make mankind in Our image, according to Our likeness" (Gen. 1:26). God made man in his image, not in the image of angels.

4. The Tanakh emphasizes that God is first and foremost a Father (Jer. 31:9; Deut. 1:21; 8:5; Ex. 4:22; Isa. 1:2). Since God is not dependent on creation to be who he is, the Son must be eternal as well. The Spirit of God is understood to be one with God but also distinct from the Father and the Son (Isa. 48:16).

Part 2: Didn't Yeshua Take Away from the Law?

1. The Tanakh taught that after Israel broke the first covenant, the Messiah would initiate the beginning of a new covenant (Josh. 7:11; Hos. 8:1; Ezek. 16:59).
    a. We should expect, then, that when we are under the new covenant, we are no longer under the old covenant
    b. This is exactly what the New Testament teaches: that the old covenant laws actually all functioned to foreshadow the Messiah, Yeshua. (Col. 2:17)
    c. The old covenant laws further served to set the people

apart for God. But what now sets God's people apart is God's Spirit dwelling inside them. (Lev. 19:2; 20:7–8; Ex. 19:5; 1 Peter 1:2)
   d. Under the new covenant we are no longer bound to the laws of the Torah. If we have come into the new covenant by receiving Christ, we won't receive the curse of disobeying the Torah, which is death and separation from God. However, we are still sinning if we break the law, because we are going against God's good character

Part 3: Virgins Can't Give Birth

1. If there really is an extremely powerful, uncaused, eternal being who created the universe, then this being would certainly be able to enter into his own creation without being governed by the rules of that creation.

2. The virgin birth is one such miracle. If God exists, then causing a virgin birth would be child's play for him (Gen. 18:14).

3. The theme of miraculous birth is common in the story of the Jewish people. It doesn't appear out of the blue with the Messiah (Gen. 25:21; 29:31; 30:22–23).

4. Prophecy told us that the Messiah would be born from a virgin (Isa. 7:14). And in every other use of *almah*, the Hebrew word used by Isaiah, it is translated "virgin."

Part 4: How Could Yeshua Be the Son of David?

Several prophecies make it clear the Messiah must be a descendant of David.

1. Objection: Yeshua couldn't be a descendant of David if he had no earthly father.
   a. Jewish culture has always considered legal fathers the authentic fathers in every respect. There is even a biblical

precedent for this in Jacob's adoption of Joseph's sons (Gen. 48:4–6).

2. Later Rabbinical Objection: Joseph wasn't Yeshua's father.
   a. Genealogical scrolls were readily available in the temple, where many of Yeshua's accusers worked. Although they accused him of many things, none of their accusations were about not coming from the line of David
   a. People only started to claim Yeshua wasn't from the line of David long after the scrolls were destroyed.

3. Later Rabbinical Objection: The New Testament genealogies contradict themselves.
   a. The genealogy in Matthew records Yeshua's connection to King David through his legal father's line.
   b. The genealogy in Luke records Yeshua's connection to King David through his mother's line.
   c. On his legal father's side, Yeshua came through the line of Jeconiah, who was cursed to have no descendants on the throne. But God delights in forgiving and undoing curses. In Haggai 2:23, God reversed the curse Jeconiah brought on his descendants

Part 5: Why Isn't There Peace?

Prophecy makes it clear that the Messiah is supposed to bring peace.

1. The Messianic promise of peace is more than just world peace. It's personal and relational peace, peace with nature, and first and foremost, peace with God. It's about restoring us to the peace we had in the garden of Eden.
   a. We can only experience any of the other kinds of peace when we have peace with God.
   b. The garden of Eden peace can only be restored by undoing the curse Adam and Eve brought to creation.

2. Yeshua will reign over the earth, and his kingdom will be at

peace (Isa. 2:1–4; 9:7).
a. There's no world peace yet because God, in his mercy, is delaying separating the wicked from his good creation, giving all people every opportunity to follow him. But he won't delay forever (Mal. 4:1–3; Ps. 1:4–6; Heb. 10:37).

Conclusion

This book is not intended as an attack on the Jewish people. Far the opposite. It is written by a Jew who loves his people and whose heart breaks for them because he's convinced God loves the Jewish people. He wants them to know him personally. Yet they have no true relationship with the God of Israel or understanding of his good purposes for them because they've been misguided and prevented from seeing that purpose, primarily through the myth of the oral Torah. So, this Jew is trying to give back the authentic guide to the Jewish people, the Bible.

By now I hope you have seen sufficient evidence that rabbinical Judaism—as it is practiced today—is not truly Jewish, and that most things associated with Jewishness today are man-made traditions, not from the God they claim to come from. I hope you also have sufficient evidence that the God of Israel did root the Jewish people in the written Tanakh and that the Tanakh teaches the true Jewish way of life. The Jewish way of life the Tanakh teaches is to enjoy the free gift of life by receiving the Messiah Yeshua and placing your faith in him.

If you want to follow Yeshua, that's amazing! You can start by telling God that you know you are a sinner and ask him for forgiveness. Tell him you believe he died on the cross to pay for your sins and that he rose again, that you are ready to turn away from sinful patterns, and that you want to trust him with your life. I'd also encourage you to start reading God's letter to you. Some notable translations of the Bible are the NASB (used in this book), ESV, LSB, and NKJV.[1]

If you're not convinced that Yeshua is the Messiah, thank you for reading this far. I seriously respect your openmindedness. If you're at least intrigued by some of what you've read, I'd encourage you to pick up a good translation of the Tanakh, and just read through it to see what you notice. I would recommend Robert Alter's translation; it is a good secular translation that has won awards from both Jewish and Christian groups.

> "Jesus said to him, 'I am the way, and the truth, and the life.
>
> No one comes to the Father except through me.'" (John 14:6)

Request for the Reader

Thank you for reading my book! I love my people and I know God loves them too and wants them to know him personally. Please leave an honest review for this book on Amazon. That will help this book gain exposure so it can hopefully introduce more people to the Messiah, Yeshua. I will personally read every review and be super-appreciative.

Learn more and get connected at TheTorahGuide.com.

How to Find References

1. Bible references: All Bible citations are in-text citations. All Bible quotes are in the NASB version. If you don't have access to a physical Bible, you can use an online resource like Biblegateway.com, Biblehub.com, Youversion Bible app, or Sefaria.
   a. For a resource to check the Hebrew for yourself, you can use Biblehub.com. Use the search bar to find the book chapter and verse, then click "int." That will show you the Hebrew words below the English, and if you click on the Hebrew, it will show you definitions.
2. Oral Torah references: Almost all oral Torah references are in-text citations. If you're unfamiliar with oral Torah, a good resource available to use is Sefaria. Sefaria is a free, Jewish-run online library of Jewish texts.
3. Ancient primary sources: The ancient, quoted sources are public domain and can be found with a quick google search of the historian and title of the work.
4. The rest of the sources are from various books, lectures or interviews that can be found either online, in libraries, or on YouTube.

Bibliography

Alter, Robert. *The Art of Biblical Narrative*. New York, NY: Basic Books, 2011.

Alter, Robert. *The Hebrew Bible: A Translation with Commentary*. 1. Vol. 1. 3 vols. New York, NY: W. W. Norton & Company, 2019.

Bar, Eitan, and Golan Broshi. *Rabbinic Judaism Debunked*. One for Israel Ministry, 2019.

Bar, Eitan. *Refuting Rabbinic Objections to Christianity and Messianic Prophecies*. One for Israel Ministry, 2019.

Bar, Dr. Eitan. "The Talmud (Rabbinic Tradition) vs. the New Testament." ONE FOR ISRAEL Ministry, October 27, 2021.

Biswaswas, Saugato. "A Curious Case of Sweating Blood." *Indian Journal of Dermatology*, 2013.

Brustein, William I., and Ryan D. King. "Anti-Semitism in Europe before the Holocaust." *International Political Science Review / Revue Internationale de Science Politique* 25, no. 1 (2004): 35–53. http://www.jstor.org/stable/1601621.

Cain, S. , Stendahl, . Krister , Davis, . H. Grady , Sander, . Emilie T. , Bruce, . Frederick Fyvie , Flusser, . David , Fredericksen, . Linwood, Rylaarsdam, . J. Coert , Faherty, . Robert L. , Grant, . Robert M. and Sarna, . Nahum M.. "biblical literature." Encyclopedia Britannica, February 26, 2021. "Committee on Jewish Law and Standards," n.d. Accessed 2022.

Corinaldi, Michael. *Jewish Identity: The Case of Ethiopian Jewry*. Jerusalem, Israel: Magnes Press, Hebrew University, 1998.

Ehrhardt, A. "The Birth of the Synagogue and R. Akiba." *Studia Theologica - Nordic Journal of Theology* 9, no. 1 (1955): 86–111. https://doi.org/10.1080/00393385508599760.

Elazar, Daniel J. "LAND, STATE AND DIASPORA IN THE HISTORY OF THE JEWISH POLITY." *Jewish Political Studies Review* 3, no. 1/2 (1991): 3–31. http://www.jstor.org/stable/25834195.

Foley, J. Miles. "oral tradition." Encyclopedia Britannica, January 6, 2019.

Flavius, Josephus. *The Wars of the Jews or History of the Destruction of Jerusalem*. Translated by William Whiston. *Gutenberg*. Project Gutenberg, 2009.

"Genealogy." GENEALOGY - JewishEncyclopedia.com. Accessed February 19, 2022. https://www.jewishencyclopedia.com/articles/6577-genealogy.

Gilbert, Greg. *Why Trust the Bible?* Wheaton, IL: Crossway, 2015.

Gruber, Daniel. *Rabbi Akiba's Messiah: The Origins of Rabbinic Authority*. Hanover, NH: Elijah Publishing, 1999.

H., Wright Christopher J. *The Mission of God: Unlocking the Bible's Grand Narrative*. Downers Grove, IL: IVP Academic, 2008.

Heschel, Abraham Joshua. *God in Search of Man: A Philosophy of Judaism*. New York, NY: Farrar, Straus and Giroux, 2000.

Irenaeus, and Philip Schaff. *Against Heresies*. Moscow, ID: Roman Roads Media, 2015.

Jocz, Jakob. *The Spiritual History of Israel*. Digital 2019ed. London: Eyre & Spottiswoode, 1961.

Kendall, R. T., and David Rosen. *The Christian and the Pharisee: Two Outspoken Religious Leaders Debate the Road to Heaven*. New York, New York: Faith Words, 2007.

Lazerwitz, Bernard, J. Alan Winter, Arnold Dashefsky, and Ephraim Tabory. *Jewish Choices: American Jewish Denominationalism.* Albany, N.Y: State University of New York Press, 1998.

Mackie, Tim. "How Jesus and the Apostles Read Their Bibles." Class Lecture. Introduction to the Hebrew Bible, BibleProject Classroom.

Mccarter, P. Kyle, Nahum M Sarna, Joseph A Callaway, Andre Lemaire, Siegfried H Horn, James D Purvis, Lee I. A. Levine, and Shaye J. D. Cohen. *Ancient Israel: A Short History from Abraham to the Roman Destruction of the Temple.* Edited by Hershel Shanks. Washington, D.C: Biblical Archaeology Society, 2008.

McDowell, Sean Joslin. "A Historical Evaluation of the Evidence for the Death of the Apostles as Martyrs for Their Faith," 2015.

Miller, Chaim. *Torah, the Five Books of Moses: With Complete Haftarah Cycle.* Brooklyn, NY: Lifestyle Books, 2011.

Nadler, Sam. *The Messianic Answer Book: Jewish Answers to Jewish Questions about the Jewish Messiah.* Charlotte, NC: Word of Messiah Ministries, 2008.

"O.T. Names of God - Study Resources." Blue Letter Bible, n.d. Accessed January 19, 2022.

Reeves, Michael. *Delighting in the Trinity: An Introduction to the Christian Faith.* Downers Grove, Illinois: IVP Academic, 2012.

Robinson John A.T. *The Human Face of God.* Philadelphia, PA: Westminster Press, 1973.

Seeman, Don. "ETHNOGRAPHERS, RABBIS AND JEWISH EPISTEMOLOGY: THE CASE OF THE ETHIOPIAN JEWS." *Tradition: A Journal of Orthodox Jewish Thought* 25, no. 4 (1991): 13–29. http://www.jstor.org/stable/23260928.

Scott, J. Julius. *Jewish Backgrounds of the New Testament.* Grand Rapids, MI: Baker Books, 2003.

Sherwin-White, Adrian N. *Roman Society and Roman Law in the New Testament*. Oxford: Clarendon Press, 1963.

Shinan, Avigdor. פרוספור שנא) נוא' תירבעה) םודה: הכלהה לש זח"ל איננה מהתנ"ך!!! Other. *YouTube,* January 14, 2016. https://www.youtube.com/watch?v=D5N4pB2KI0c.

Skolnik, Fred, ed. *Encyclopaedia Judaica*. 22 vols. Farmington Hills, MI: Keter Publishing House, 2007.

Speiser, E. A. "Ṭwṭpt." *The Jewish Quarterly Review* 48, no. 2 (1957): 370. https://doi.org/10.2307/1452711.

Strobel, Lee. *The Case for Christ*. Grand Rapids, Michigan: Zondervan Publishing, 1998.

Tacitus, Cornelius, William Jackson Brodribb, and Sara Bryant. "The Annals: 15.44." Essay. In *The Complete Works of Tacitus,* translated by Alfred John Church. New York, NY: Randomhouse Inc, 1942.

"The Talmud." Reform Judaism. Accessed January 18, 2022. https://reformjudaism.org/talmud.

Weitzman, Steven P, and R. Timothy Debold. "The Second Temple Period," 2021.

Yamauchi, Edwin M. *The World of the First Christians*. Tring, Hertfordshire: Lion, 1982.

Endnotes

Chapter 1: The Function of the Written Torah in Jewish Identity

1 Daniel J. Elazar, "Land, State and Diaspora in the History of the Jewish Polity," *Jewish Political Studies Review* 3, no. 1/2 (1991): 3. http://www.jstor.org/stable/25834195.
2 William I. Brustein and Ryan D. King, "Anti-Semitism in Europe before the Holocaust," *International Political Science Review / Revue Internationale de Science Politique* 25, no. 1 (2004): 35–36, http://www.jstor.org/stable/1601621.
3 P. Kyle McCarter et al., *Ancient Israel: A Short History from Abraham to the Roman Destruction of the Temple*, ed. Hershel Shanks (Biblical Archaeology Society, 1988), 16-19.
4 Abraham J Heschel, *A Philosophy of Judaism*, (New York: Farrar, Straus and Giroux, 2000), 167
5 Elazar, "Land,"4.
6 McCarter, *Ancient Israel*, 16–19.
7 Christopher J.H Wright, *The Mission of God: Unlocking the Bible's Grand Narrative*, (Downers Grove, IL: IVP Academic, 2008), 65.
8 Robert Alter, *The Hebrew Bible: A Translation with Commentary*, vol 1 (New York: W. W. Norton, 2019), 40–41.
9 P. Kyle McCarter et al., *Ancient Israel: A Short History from Abraham to the Roman Destruction of the Temple*, ed. Hershel Shanks (Biblical Archaeology Society, 1988), 153–54.
10 Alter, *Hebrew Bible*, 617.

Chapter 2: Origins of Rabbinic Judaism

1 Julius J. Scott, *Jewish Backgrounds of the New Testament* (Grand Rapids:

Baker, 2003), 201.

2 R.T. Kendall and David Rosen, *The Christian and the Pharisee* (New York: Faith Words, 2007), 7.

3 Fred Skolnik and Michael Berenbaum, *Encyclopaedia Judaica*, vol. 13 (Farmington Hills, MI: Macmillan Reference in assoc. with the Keter, 2007), 85–86.

4 Fred Skolnik and Michael Berenbaum, *Encyclopaedia Judaica*, vol. 16 (Farmington Hills, MI: Macmillan Reference USA, 2007), 30.

5 Eitan Bar and Golan Broshi, *Rabbinic Judaism Debunked*, (One for Israel Ministry, 2019), 12.

6 Josephus Flavius, *The Wars of the Jews or History of the Destruction of Jerusalem*, trans. William Whiston(Project Gutenberg, 2009), 1.5.2.

7 A. Ehrhardt, "The Birth of the Synagogue and R. Akiba," *Studia Theologica—Nordic Journal of Theology* 9, no. 1 (1955): pp. 86–111, https://doi.org/10.1080/00393385508599760, 95–97.

8 Hershel Shanks et al, eds. *Ancient Israel: A Short History from Abraham to the Roman Destruction of the Temple* (Washington D.C., Biblical Archaeology Society, 2008,) 185.

9 Flavius, *The Wars of the Jews*, 1.5.2

10 Flavius, *Antiquities*, 13.10.6.

11 Bar, *Rabbinic Judaism Debunked*, 12

12 Fred Skolnik and Michael Berenbaum, *Encyclopaedia Judaica*, vol. 18 (Farmington Hills, MI: Macmillan Reference USA, 2007), 21–22.

13 Scott, *Jewish Backgrounds of the New Testament*, 172.

14 Flavius, *Antiquities*, 13.10.6.

15 Moses Maimonides, 1470, *Mishneh Torah*, Transmission of the Oral Law.

16 Fred Skolnik and Michael Berenbaum, *Encyclopaedia Judaica*, vol. 15 (Farmington Hills, MI: Macmillan Reference USA, 2007), 456.

17 Skolnik, *Encyclopaedia Judaica*, vol. 19, 486.

18 Maimonides, *Mishneh Torah*, Transmission of the Oral Law.

19 Skolnik, *Encyclopaedia Judaica*, vol. 14, 321–.22.

20 Skolnik, *Encyclopaedia Judaica*, vol. 19, 470.

21 Skolnik, *Encyclopaedia Judaica*, vol. 7, 423.

22 Kendall and Rosen, *The Christian and the Pharisee*, 7.

23 IGod.co.il, פרוספור ואנש (נוא' עהרבעית) הדום: הכלהה של זח"ל הנניא המהתנ"ך!!!,

YouTube Video, 8:04. January 14, 2016, https://www.youtube.com/watch?v=D5N4pB2KI0c.

24 Eitan Bar, "The Talmud (Rabbinic Tradition) vs. the New Testament," One for Israel Ministry, October 27, 2021.

25 E. A. Speiser, "Ṭwṭpt," *The Jewish Quarterly Review* 48, no. 2 (1957): 370, https://doi.org/10.2307/1452711.

26 Edwin M. Yamauchi, *The World of the First Christians* (Tring, Hertfordshire: Lion., 1982), 18.

27 Chaim Miller, *Torah, the Five Books of Moses: With Complete Haftarah Cycle,* (Brooklyn: Lifestyle Books, 2011), 9–11.

28 Bernard Melvin Lazerwitz et al., *Jewish Choices: American Jewish Denominationalism* (Albany, NY: State Univ. of New York Press, 1998), 15.

29 Lazerwitz et al., *Jewish Choices: American Jewish Denominationalism,* 16.

30 Lazerwitz et al., *Jewish Choices: American Jewish Denominationalism,* 17.

31 "The Talmud," Reform Judaism, accessed March 5, 2022, https://reformjudaism.org/talmud.

32 Skolnik, *Encyclopaedia Judaica,* vol. 17, 173.

33 Lazerwitz et al., *Jewish Choices: American Jewish Denominationalism,* 21.

34 Skolnik, *Encyclopaedia Judaica,* vol. 5, 174.

Chapter 3: The Oral Torah Examined

1 Jakob Jocz, *The Spiritual History of Israel,* (London: Eyre & Spottiswoode, 1961,) Retrieved from https://jocz.ca/wp-content/uploads/2019/10/THE-SPIRITUAL-HISTORY-OF-ISRAEL.pdf, 104.

2 Skolnik, *Encyclopaedia Judaica,* vol. 11, 665.

3 Skolnik, *Encyclopaedia Judaica,* vol. 11, 665.

4 J. Miles Foley, "Oral Tradition," *Encyclopedia Britannica,* January 6, 2019.

5 Foley, "Oral Tradition," *Encyclopedia Britannica.*

6 Fred Skolnik and Michael Berenbaum, *Encyclopaedia Judaica,* vol. 19 (Farmington Hills, MI: Macmillan Reference USA, 2007), 470.

7 Robert Alter, *The Art of Biblical Narrative,* (New York: Basic Books, 2011), 12.

8 Bar, *Rabbinic Judaism Debunked,* 91.

9 Corinaldi Michael, *Jewish Identity: The Case of Ethiopian Jewry* (Jerusalem:

Hebrew University Magnes Press, 1998), 46-50.

10 Corinaldi, *Jewish Identity: Ethiopian Jewry*, 48–49.

11 Don Seeman, "Ethnographers, Rabbis and Jewish Epistemology: The Case of the Ethiopian Jews," *Tradition: A Journal of Orthodox Jewish Thought* 25, no. 4 (1991): 13–29, http://www.jstor.org/stable/23260928.

Chapter 4: Judaism According to the Tanakh

1 Fred Skolnik and Michael Berenbaum, *Encyclopaedia Judaica*, vol. 3 (Farmington Hills, MI: Macmillan Reference USA, 2007), 578.

2 Skolnik, *Encyclopaedia Judaica*, vol. 11. 126.

3 Jakob Jocz, *The Spiritual History of Israel*, (London: Eyre & Spottiswoode, 1961,) retrieved from https://jocz.ca/wp-content/uploads/2019/10/the-spiritual-history-of-israel.pdf, 102.

Chapter 5: The Tanakh and the New Testament

1 Sam Nadler, *The Messianic Answer Book: Jewish Answers to Jewish Questions about the Jewish Messiah*, (Charlotte, NC: Word of Messiah Ministries, 2008), 79.

2 Craig L. Blomberg, *The Historical Reliability of the Gospels* (Downers Grove, IL: IVP Academic, 2007), 249–51.

3 Sean Joslin McDowell, "A Historical Evaluation of the Evidence for the Death of the Apostles as Martyrs for Their Faith" (dissertation, 2015), 2–4.

4 Greg Gilbert, *Why Trust the Bible?* (Wheaton, IL: Crossway, 2015), 84.

5 Irenaeus and Philip Schaff, *Against Heresies* (Moscow, ID: Roman Roads Media, 2015), 5.

6 Richard Bauckham, *Jesus and the Eyewitnesses: The Gospels as Eyewitness Testimony* (Grand Rapids: Eerdmans, 2017), 7-8.

7 McDowell, "Apostles as Martyrs," 426–28.

8 Saugato Biswaswas, "A Curious Case of Sweating Blood." *Indian Journal of Dermatology* (2013,) 478–80.

9 Lee Strobel, *The Case for Christ*, (Grand Rapids: Zondervan, 1998)35.

10 McDowell, "Apostles as Martyrs," 27-29.

11 John A. T. Robinson, *The Human Face of God* (Philadelphia: Westminster,

1973), 131.

12 Fred Skolnik and Michael Berenbaum, *Encyclopaedia Judaica*, vol. 18 (Farmington Hills, MI: Macmillan Reference USA, 2007), 307

13 Tim Mackie, "How Jesus and the Apostles Read Their Bibles" (Class Lecture, Introduction to the Hebrew Bible, BibleProject Classroom).

14 Nadler, *The Messianic Answer Book*, 12

Chapter 6: Common Concerns

1 Michael Reeves, *Delighting in the Trinity: An Introduction to the Christian Faith* (Downers Grove, Illinois: IVP Academic, 2012,) 24.

2 Nadler, *The Messianic Answer book*, 57. [Complete pub info, please.]

3 Eitan Bar, *Refuting Rabbinic Objections to Christianity and Messianic Prophecies* (One for Israel Ministry, 2019), 123.

4 JewishEncyclopedia.com, s.v., "genealogy," accessed March 10, 2022, https://www.jewishencyclopedia.com/articles/6577-genealogy.

Conclusion

1 Abbreviations for the New American Standard Bible (NASB), English Standard Version (ESV), Legacy Standard Bible (LSB), and New King James Version (NKJV).

Printed in Great Britain
by Amazon